TeamWork

Setting the Standard for Collaborative Teaching, Grades 5-9

TeamWork

Setting the Standard
for Collaborative Teaching,
Grades 5-9

Monique D. Wild
Amanda S. Mayeaux
Kathryn P. Edmonds

Foreword by Jack C. Berckemeyer

Stenhouse Publishers
Portland, Maine

National Middle School Association
Westerville, Ohio

Stenhouse Publishers
www.stenhouse.com

National Middle School Association
www.nmsa.org

Library of Congress Cataloging-in-Publication Data

Wild, Monique D.
  Teamwork : setting the standard for collaborative teaching, grades 5-9 /
  Monique D. Wild, Amanda S. Mayeaux, Kathryn P. Edmonds.
      p. cm.
  Includes bibliographical references and index.
  ISBN 978-1-57110-711-4 (alk. paper)
  1. Team learning approach in education. I. Mayeaux, Amanda S. II.
  Edmonds, Kathryn P. III. Title.

LB1032.W54 2008
371.14'8--dc22

                                        2007040718

Cover, interior design, and typesetting by Designboy Creative Group

Manufactured in the United States of America on acid-free, recycled paper
14 13 12 11 10 09 08   9 8 7 6 5 4 3 2

To our students—past, present, and future

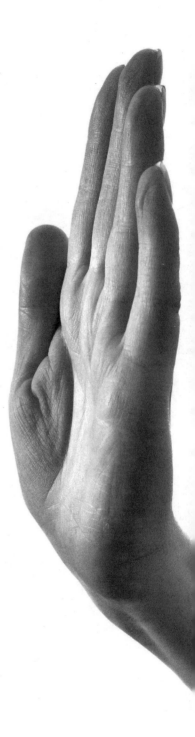

You've learned the things you need

To pass that test and many more—

I'm certain you'll succeed.

We've taught you that the earth is round,

That red and white make pink,

And something else that matters more—

We've taught you how to think.

~Hooray for Diffendoofer Day!
by Dr. Seuss, Jack Prelutsky, and Lane Smith

Contents

Foreword

For several years I was fortunate to serve as a judge for the Disney American Teacher Awards. I can still remember the countless hours I spent reading applications. Every once in a while I'd come across one that stood out from the field of incredible teachers. This was how I discovered the amazing work that Monique Wild, Amanda Mayeaux, and Kathryn Edmonds were doing in Louisiana. They went on to win the Disney award in 2006, becoming the first team to earn the national "Teacher of the Year" designation.

I am honored to write the foreword to their first book. These teachers show how important it is to be a great team. They paint a visual wonderland of their classrooms where they demonstrate how teachers can truly make a difference in the lives of young adolescents. I so admire the dedication and commitment that each of these outstanding educators has shown for her school and her students.

What a great journey these middle-level educators have taken. As many of you are aware, teaming often feels like the topsy-turvy whirl of the wild teacup ride at Disney's theme parks. Sometimes the experience is like a trip to Space Mountain. You move into the dark, your head spins, and you reach a peak only to be jolted back down as the ride hits new twists and curves.

These authors have lived through that turbulence and hold nothing back in their descriptions. They have earned the right to brag a little about their many successes. But what resonates most is their honesty in sharing the struggles, conflicts, and disagreements that helped them grow and endure.

Wild, Mayeaux, and Edmonds also share a critical lesson regarding the realities of the No Child Left Behind Act. In an age of accountability, these teachers embrace the constant changes and respond with innovation. They work together to plan interdisciplinary units that are motivating to young adolescents but still tied to state standards. Never once do they use the challenge of standards to settle for mediocre lessons. This is an important life lesson for all middle-level educators.

Administrators also should note how these teachers use their team time effectively. They divide and conquer tasks for efficiency while holding each other accountable for results. The teammates share sound strategies for establishing policies and procedures and involving others in their work. I encourage you to review their record of success in building relationships and communicating with parents.

Whether you are an experienced teacher or new to the field, you will be inspired by how this team puts the principles of National Middle School Association's *This We Believe* (2003) into action. Every team in the middle grades should adopt their approach. As you will soon discover, these teammates are devoted to their students and have significant knowledge to share about young adolescents and their healthy academic, emotional, and social development.

Because these three teachers are so accomplished, their ideas and suggestions may seem overwhelming to those who are just starting. Keep in mind that the authors developed these best practices over time. By their own admission, they were not an overnight sensation. My advice is to select several of the strategies they offer, implement and refine them, and keep adding layers over time. Focus on continual improvement, not immediate perfection. Follow their path and you may discover that your own team's dreams will come true.

Jack C. Berckemeyer

Assistant Executive Director, National Middle School Association

Acknowledgments

We would like to acknowledge the 2006 Disney American Teacher Awards selection committee, led by Terry Wick, for giving us the opportunity to share our passion for teaching with educators around the world. Furthermore, we'd like to thank the Disney Corporation for recognizing excellence in teaching for more than seventeen years. We are also grateful to our fellow Disney teacher honorees for their continued inspiration and motivation.

We are especially indebted to Doug Walker, Susan Jordan, and Cathy Meredith for trusting us enough to let us teach; to the Ascension Parish school system for creating a culture that continuously strives to meet students' needs in an ever-changing world; and to the teachers at Dutchtown Middle School for the unbelievable opportunity to teach the Challenge program with their support. Erin Babin, Katie Sheffield, Debbie Vicknair, Larry Chambless, Angie Gaudin, Rebecca Acosta, Christine Wood, Becky Petite, and Pat Mouton all were part of our team at some point and taught us to love kids without limits. Our appreciation would not be complete without acknowledging our students' parents, who have supported our crazy ideas during the past seven years.

We feel blessed by the presence of Holly Holland, who saw three weeping women accept an award and envisioned the potential that became this book. Her guidance, honesty, and directness made a difficult process quite an enjoyable experience.

We approached writing this book as a team, but we also would like to express our gratitude individually.

Monique: I am thankful for the support of my husband and two children, who contributed to this book by cooking meals, completing household chores, and tolerating the glow of the computer screen on family movie nights. You make life a joyous adventure every day. I would also like to thank my parents and grandparents for making learning an enjoyable experience. It is because of them that I continue to seek knowledge and share it with others.

Amanda: To my husband, who is the quiet giant in my life, slaying all of my fears and pushing on to forgotten dreams uttered in youth, I love you beyond words. To our daughters, you are strong women in the making, and we are so proud of you. Thank you for sharing your mommy with others. To my parents, who took me around the world and created a fearless woman, thank you. To my support group—Vanessa, my in-laws, and my sister—thank you for the hours and hours of babysitting that allowed the book to be born.

Finally, to Jesus Christ, my Light and my Salvation, may I always be what you willed me to be.

Kathryn: Thank you to my husband and best friend, the one person who has enough strength to love me, support me, encourage me, and still have the energy to make me laugh. Thanks to my parents, grandparents, and family for giving me roots, wings, and the wisdom to know when to stay grounded and when to soar. Thank you to my fabulous friends for the number of times you stood by me, stood behind me, and lifted me up. How could I be so lucky? To Jesus Christ, from whom all my blessings have come.

Introduction
Taking a Giant Step Forward

"We are *not* babies, you know!" exclaimed Adam. "We know a giant did not come into this classroom!"

"Yeah," Brayden said. "We can see the staples [on the walls]. Besides, footprints are not made of paper, and how did he get his foot on the ceiling anyway? Did you lock the doors last night?"

Despite being outraged that they couldn't figure out who or what had left behind so many odd signs at school, the students remained fascinated by the mysterious overnight visitor to our seventh-grade classrooms. The giant had scattered messages as well as evidence of where he had been. For four days, new clues appeared throughout the team area, providing further intrigue about the nocturnal hauntings. Students begged us for information about the intruder.

Our team of teachers feigned ignorance, but behind the scenes we continued planning and collaborating to incorporate the giant into the week's lessons. Because each of us is responsible for a comprehensive required curriculum—it is prescribed down to the activities we must teach and the order in which we must cover them during a given grading period—we seized the chance to be creative.

Adam was right. Our students are not babies. But that doesn't mean they don't like to play. Young adolescents are capable of exhibiting mature behavior and deep thinking, but they still want to have fun. As they move through the transitions from childhood to adulthood, they need regular opportunities to become actively engaged in learning. So we tried to tie our required academic standards to an imaginative, energetic, and academically rigorous adventure suited to the unique persona of middle school students.

Throughout the week our students completed giant-related activities addressing curriculum requirements in each subject area. For example, they read *Jack and the Beanstalk* in language arts and discussed the elements of fantasy and fairy tales. In math they measured the footprints and handprints left by the giant and used ratio and proportion to determine the creature's actual size. The drawings they made in math class cycled back to language arts, where students wrote descriptive paragraphs containing figurative language, including metaphors and similes, for the criminal lineup of potential giant suspects. In American history, students continued to learn about the Revolutionary War. Although we designed each lesson to address the curriculum objectives, we also tried to spark the students' natural curiosity through mystery and intrigue. Middle school students love to pretend, but make-believe activities in the classroom must include higher-level thinking to stimulate them intellectually as well as emotionally.

Finally, a few students noticed that a handprint was placed directly over a map of the thirteen colonies in the history classroom. They added this clue to others, such as the note on the board that said, "Fe, fie, foe, fum, I smell the blood of freedom."

"I think the giant is searching for something to do with the Revolutionary War," Regan suggested. "Do y'all think that could be it? I mean, there's the freedom message and the hand. Maybe it's King George! Could the king be the giant?"

The next day when students entered their history classroom, each desk contained a tea bag and a message: "Here's your tea, now where's my tax?" Immediately, students began to yell, "It is the king! We knew it!"

This activity could have been the death of the giant metaphor, but because of our extensive planning and collaboration, we had more in store for our students. History teacher Erin Babin, a member of our teaching team, revealed that the giant was indeed a symbol of King George III and the British government. The day's history activities purposefully guided our students to the discovery that when the American colonists overthrew the British government during the Revolutionary War, they beat the world's military giant and planted the seeds of freedom. Although the activities led students to this realization, they earned the knowledge themselves. Each student had successfully solved the mystery. At the end of the week, we distributed the "seeds of freedom" and some dirt in which to plant them. The students returned to school with the seeds after they had sprouted a few weeks later. We used the plants in a related science activity and later placed them in our team garden.

In Part II of this book, we will revisit the dynamics of curriculum integration in more detail. For now, the message we want to send is that energetic, innovative, and collaborative teaching is alive in middle-level classrooms. And the secret weapon is teamwork.

Admittedly, providing interdisciplinary instruction in an era of high-stakes accountability can seem like a monumental undertaking. Like our colleagues around the country, we continually struggle with directives that threaten to suck the imagination out of our teaching. Although we understand the push for consistent results in all schools for all students, we don't believe in rigidity. Teamwork enables us to strike a balance—it provides the space to infuse our lessons with creative and challenging content as well as the structure to meet the requirements of state and national standards, benchmarks, and testing.

Better Together Than Alone

Teaching can be a lonely profession. This might seem like an odd statement considering the continual parade of students entering and exiting our classrooms. However, when the bell rings, signaling the end of the school day, many teachers have to savor the successes and reflect on the failures alone. When most of our work occurs in isolation behind closed doors, we miss out on the collegial exchanges that can invigorate our instruction and help us evolve, professionally and personally.

"Before I began teaming, I worked with colleagues, but only in the most superficial sense. We each worked at the same school, but we each did our own jobs," Erin Babin said, reflecting on the benefits of interdisciplinary instruction. "Collaboration has allowed me to grow professionally in ways that could not have been accomplished by any other means. I see the big picture. This has impacted student learning more dramatically than any other accomplishment in my experience with teaching."

Whether you are fresh out of college or a seasoned veteran, you will find that teamwork provides a powerful foundation for professional collaboration and high achievement. Through teamwork, veterans become energized by the exuberance of new teachers who are bursting with ideas for innovative curricular connections. Novice teachers, in turn, reap the benefits of working with experienced educators who can provide sound advice about instructional pacing, classroom management, and other fundamental skills they've refined over time.

As members of an interdisciplinary middle school team, our roles are often fluid. We respect each other enough to know that each of us has strengths and weaknesses. For example, Amanda does not have great organizational skills, but she is very good at managing instructional time allotted for special projects, so we usually call on her to create schedules. Math is not Monique's forte, but she often critiques word problems for fluency. Neither Amanda nor Monique is good at keeping up with the various forms and records required of teachers. However, Kathryn fills this void beautifully. The strongest collaboration comes when we realize how much each of us can contribute to the greater good.

We were lucky to have found each other. Amanda and Monique both began teaching about fifteen years ago at Dutchtown Middle School in Geismar, Louisiana. Two people could not be more different. Amanda was reared in five countries on four continents. The cultural diversity she experienced ranged from small-town America to the Middle East. Monique grew up near Dutchtown, as did her parents, grandparents, and great-grandparents. Although we saw the world differently, we shared a common philosophy about learning, teaching, and children. Continual reflection on the teaching craft led Monique and Amanda to attain certification from the National Board for Professional Teaching Standards in 1999 and 2002 respectively.

Kathryn joined us during the 2005–2006 school year. Growing up in a military family, she also moved quite often during her childhood. When she found a job at Dutchtown after graduating from college, she was filled with purpose. Because of her background in special education, Kathryn helped us improve the way we assisted students with learning disabilities. Kathryn is such a talented, quick starter that she has been nominated as Dutchtown's Teacher of the Year each year of her employment.

Our enthusiasm for working together inspired us to take risks, analyze our successes and failures, and seek more opportunities to learn—the same qualities we want to develop in our students. In 2006 we received the Disney American Teacher of the Year award, the first time the top prize had been given to a teaching team instead of to an individual instructor. We were so grateful for the award and the professional opportunities that followed, but we most appreciated the recognition of our work together. Suddenly we had a national platform to speak about the power of collaborative instruction.

Although our teaming experiences have transformed our professional lives, every day doesn't sparkle. Choruses of angels do not break into song when we enter the classroom. We are not perfect, nor do we have ideal teaching assignments. We cry, sigh, shout, and feel overworked. We struggle to reach difficult students, and our interventions sometimes flop. We have survived the parent/teacher conference from hell that resulted in police officers being called to school. One restraining order later, we decided our communication skills could use some work.

We also know that teachers can't always choose ideal colleagues. We've lost and gained team members over the years and encountered unsettling administrative changes that caused us to adjust our teaming methods to fit the distinct characteristics—good and bad—of each situation. Middle schools evolve year to year, and so must we. Change does not come easily to us. We all have days that make us wonder whether we should return for the next class period. However, what brings us back is the belief that all the stars eventually will align so that every one of our students will experience explosive learning. Such moments erase the pain of a thousand headaches. What we have discovered is that when we work together as a collaborative instructional team, success occurs much more frequently than when we work alone.

When we won the Disney Award, we were the members of a three-person instructional team. However, we have worked with various team configurations and have seen the addition and departure of several team members throughout the years. In the year following our recognition, Erin Babin joined our group. We are indebted to Erin and all of our previous team members. The professional relationships we developed with them have consistently strengthened us. The experiences we share in this book are the result of our work with these talented educators.

Our lives would be simpler if we would just bend to the state and district requirements and teach the curriculum in a lockstep sequence. We would not have to work so hard to find extra materials, create interdisciplinary connections, and change our initial plans because a colleague suggested a better approach. But then we would lose a valuable asset—our students' interest. We create cross-curricular links, like those formulated in our giant unit, to show students how ideas and topics connect across subjects and throughout our lives. Teamwork is the vehicle that drives this point home through fluid, relevant lessons that go beyond the basics.

Early adolescence is a crucial time in a student's life. Academic expectations increase and planning for high school, college, and careers starts to take shape, all while students are changing physically, socially, and emotionally. Their need to belong and affiliate with peers often overrides their common sense. They get distracted and become erratic. They try on and cast off roles faster than improvisational actors, and they challenge authority and perceived unfairness with passion—but not always prudence. To steer them through the storms, middle grades teachers must be both compassionate and conscientious, seeking always to understand a young adolescent's desire for a purposeful and engaging education. Interdisciplinary teaming provides an ideal framework for organizing important intellectual and life lessons.

Teachers who work on interdisciplinary teams discover that there is more than enough time to plan interesting, integrated activities, counsel students, contact parents, communicate with administrators, collaborate with other educators, and grow professionally. In short, teamwork makes it possible to wear the many hats required of teachers who interact daily with young adolescent learners.

Unfortunately, many schools and school districts quickly jump on the teaming bandwagon after limited preparation and, due to poor implementation, fail to achieve satisfactory results. Too often teamwork stops at the organizational level by placing teachers specializing in three or four core subject areas together in the same hallway of a school building. Effective interdisciplinary teams understand the job is much more complex than school structures alone. Effective teams are able to build relationships with students, families, and other professionals to advance student achievement.

"While changing and modifying organizational patterns and refining and strengthening curriculum and assessment are essential, they are not sufficient," Williamson and Johnston (1999) remind us. "Teams are not implemented just to have teams. Grouping is not modified just to have practice. Such changes take place because they contribute to greater student achievement and success" (16).

Creating a Masterpiece

We don't consider school to be an August to May routine built on standardized tests and periodic report cards. We see education as a tapestry continually created by master weavers seeking to produce the ultimate artwork, a child who unfurls to his or her greatest potential. Our team is not just a collection of individuals who teach unrelated subjects to students who move among our connected classrooms. We see ourselves as three in one—the master weaver.

How do you create a school environment that produces such works of art? That is our challenge each day as we build a world where learning is infectious, standards are surpassed, and everyone has a chance to change the world.

Our classrooms may have walls, but these physical barriers do not stop the intellectual flow from one room to the next. In our interdisciplinary team we understand that each experience throughout the day has a common link:

the thread of the children. As the master weavers, we have discovered not only how the young adolescent brain learns but also that it will change and expand more from ages ten to fourteen than at any other period of life except birth to age two. Our short time with these students will have a tremendous impact on their development and their future. Therefore, we must maximize each moment to stretch them to their emotional, social, and intellectual limits while enabling them to feel confident and successful. We have no time for frivolous lessons that lack academic substance and require little cognitive engagement. On a daily basis our students must ponder difficult questions, often with no right answers. We believe in teaching them to think, not to echo us. Yet we understand that students at this age are still children at heart and our lessons must offer intrigue mixed with amusement in order to capture their attention and maximize learning.

We also understand that others surround our loom. Families, friends, administrators, school staff, and many others play a part in this creation. The key to our success is involving all of these essential people in shaping our students.

Unlike some other books focusing on adolescent development and middle grades education, we do not seek to share prescriptive activities and lesson plans or put people to sleep with theories that have few practical applications. Instead, we offer a view of teaming that is grounded in the everyday experiences of working teachers who know what it means to cope with state and federal mandates, at-risk learners, and constant scheduling changes due to a rapidly growing school. We plan together, strive together, revise together, and write together. This book is not a step-by-step method of creating an instructional team. We realize that, just as all children are different, each team is unique. This book offers critical concepts about teaming, young adolescents, and middle grades teaching that will require the reader to reflect, adjust, and grow. We share our story to encourage other middle school teams to share theirs. Our hope is that teachers and administrators who read this book will accept our invitation to continually examine their professional practices and create learning utopias in the midst of pressure-packed standards and accountability requirements.

Great interdisciplinary teaching is not a quick fix or an easy method of instruction, regardless of what some may suggest. Great interdisciplinary teaching is a personal commitment to colleagues, students, and families, not a checklist of duties. It is child-centered, not teacher-centered. We tell our students that success is excellence every day. This book is for those who expect high achievement not only from their students but also from themselves.

In the following chapters we will share not only our successes, but also our failures. Our achievements have brought us recognition, but our setbacks have made us more reflective practitioners. The underlying magic is not how we set up our team schedule or manage a meeting. It is the energy we bring to our collegial conversations and the expectations we have personally and for each other. Teamwork enables us to dream big and then deliver on that promise.

Part 1
Strong Relationships

Before you begin this journey, close your eyes and think about the best teacher you ever had. Can you remember a specific lesson? Do you recall a special conversation the two of you shared? What did this teacher do that set him or her apart from others who contributed to your education?

When we ask colleagues these questions, they never say, "Oh, Mr. Green was the neatest lesson planner" or "Ms. Smith always made sure we sat at our desks with our feet glued to the floor."

Instead, the best teachers in our memories are those who made strong emotional connections. They touched our hearts as well as our heads. They inspired us to follow them into the profession.

On our team, the curriculum is not the central focus. We teach students first and then the content. Relationships are at the forefront of every activity, and that is true whether we are working with our students or our colleagues.

Before criticizing us for being intellectually soft or too touchy-feely, please examine the results of this approach and explore the full cycle of teaming described in this book. We have experienced great success when using teamwork to build relationships, accelerate learning in multiple dimensions, and improve our personal and professional practices. The synergy is the secret.

ChapterOne
Learning to Work with Colleagues

"You really love each other," said Lauren. "You respect each other, and you show us every day how to work together."

"We know you disagree sometimes, but you get through it. We want to be the same way with each other," other students told us.

To help us prepare for a presentation at National Middle School Association's annual conference, we invited fifteen students to Monique's house one summer afternoon so that we could interview them about effective teaming practices. Their insights caused us to revisit a topic we have debated over the years, namely whether teachers who collaborate must also be friends.

We were not buddies when we began working together, although we are now. The strong personal bonds we've formed have enriched us, to be sure, but they are not the key to our success in the classroom. Rather, respectful, trusting professional relationships are what sustain us.

"For teachers, teams provide the kind of collaborative work group that is increasingly viewed as vital to organizational productivity across a wide range of professions," Anthony Jackson and Gayle Davis write in *Turning Points 2000*. "The shared insights, critique, conjecture, search for evidence, discussion of lessons learned, prodding, probing, and small celebrations of success that permeate the conversations of effective teams are the primary means by which teachers create their professional knowledge about teaching" (128).

Establishing a collaborative working relationship begins with simple plans that all instructional teams can make to build unity. When a new team forms, members should focus on three activities — developing common goals, examining each other's core beliefs, and identifying the strengths that each person brings to the team — to set the stage for productive interactions.

Each year when we begin discussing our educational goals, we shoot for the stars. Our conversations focus on global concepts that will guide our work. Initially, we had one, broad vision: *all students will be successful*. This made sense in theory but proved difficult to quantify in practice. So we kept refining, adding layers and details that would help us hit specific targets and evaluate our progress while not losing sight of the broader mission.

One year many of our students had long histories of misbehavior in school and significantly weak reading skills. We realized that our goals for the year would have to address these deficits. So we set a very specific target for social development: We will have at least 95 percent of our students end the year with no behavior referrals. To address the poor reading skills, we decided to focus on a literacy standard from our language arts curriculum in all core subjects. We used a team target to address the dismal reading performance: All core classes will address literacy components such as reading, writing, viewing, speaking, and visually representing so that each student will improve reading comprehension and language skills as they maintain at least a C average in core subjects.

Setting goals based on student achievement is a reminder that teaming should represent more than the adoption of a common discipline plan or a series of jointly supervised fun activities. Working as a collaborative team helps us develop a systematic approach to student success.

To reach the point where we can authentically collaborate for students' benefit, we must build our team focus through open and honest dialogue. Prior to the start of each school year, we share our opinions about basic questions such as the following:

- Why did you become a teacher?
- What are the best methods of instruction to engage students?
- What is the strongest asset you bring to a team?
- What are your thoughts about the family's role in education and how we should involve them in our work?

The answers reveal the roots of our personal beliefs about education and how these beliefs might influence our decisions in the classroom. One opinion isn't necessarily better than another, but deeper understanding of what drives a person leads to mutual compassion and compatibility. Such knowledge also helps us consider multiple perspectives as we work together throughout the school year.

Developing a Common Agenda

Once we have thoroughly discussed our individual reactions to formative questions, we use the reflections to shape our team's purpose and procedures. Again, we start with a larger list and then narrow and sharpen the principle points by working in unison.

First, we each list the routines, practices, and methodologies of teaching that we consider nonnegotiable. These are the issues that define us as teachers. For example, Monique will not yield on her requirement that every student will read for forty minutes a day (twenty minutes during class and twenty minutes at home) to build fluency and comprehension. Amanda believes that every day should represent a fresh start for students, and any misbehavior from the previous day must be forgotten. Kathryn believes that the curriculum must not be dumbed down for special needs students; instead, their learning should be supported by inventive instructional strategies. If you explore similar issues with your team, you may be surprised by the number of core beliefs you have in common with your colleagues.

When our individual core beliefs do not align, we look for data to support the use of one approach over another. For example, there was a time when Monique would not accept late work. When students did not submit their assignments on time, she recorded a zero in her grade book. Monique's motivation was to instill responsibility and punctuality. Amanda preferred another approach. She allowed students to bring in work after the due date, but she deducted points in small increments for each day after the deadline.

As a team, we sought evidence of these opposite policies' impacts. We found that more of Amanda's students turned in assignments on time than Monique's, even with the threat of receiving a zero. When questioned about this, students said that if they were behind in Monique's class, they often didn't start the assignment at all because they knew they would get a zero. However, in Amanda's class they could turn in the assignment with only a slight deduction, so they usually proceeded despite feeling overwhelmed.

Clearly, Monique's plan was not having the intended effect. If not for the team's examination of core beliefs in conflict, she might never have discovered the flaws in her policy. But after reflecting on the data collected in our classes, Monique decided to change for the good of the team.

After establishing our team's core beliefs, we move toward shaping our shared purpose. We have found it helpful to restate these essential principles as "we believe" statements. The following section lists core beliefs that we have developed over the years:

Our Core Beliefs

We believe that the relationships we build with our students do not begin and end with the school day or the school calendar. We communicate with our students as soon as we receive the class roll, usually a few weeks after we have said good-bye to our previous team. We also keep in touch with students long after they leave us. In the midst of writing this chapter, we heard about a former student whose mother had died. The family decided to have a private funeral service, so we sent a card with our sympathies and our current contact information.

We believe in a student-centered environment where all children feel safe and loved. Middle school students spend most of their waking moments thinking about whether they will be accepted. With this in mind, we start building genuine relationships with and between our students from the first day of school. We make time for team activities that lead to trust and respect. We don't stop until our team becomes a cohesive unit in which all adolescents are valued for their contributions. The relationships our students develop do not end once the school year is over. One of our teams independently organized meetings after the students moved to high school so they could provide tutoring for their peers who were struggling with the transition.

We believe that school should be an equitable place where all students have opportunities to succeed. Many of our students are disadvantaged. Ensuring fairness, as Rick Wormeli (2006) points out, does not mean giving every student the same resources, instruction, or assessment. It means giving every student what he or she needs to achieve. Some may require extra time to work one-on-one with a teacher. Some may need resources their families can't afford. Some might benefit by having outside mentors, tutors, or simply a shoulder to cry on. We get to know our students as individuals; then we weave accommodations into the fabric of our team.

We believe that teaching students to take risks with their learning motivates them to tackle intellectual challenges throughout their lives. At the beginning of the school year, for example, Amanda does not count for credit the answers students provide during problem-solving workshops in math class. At first, she only grades the method they use to solve the problem, eventually building to the point when she also will consider the final answer in her grading. In this way, she encourages students to bravely tackle new concepts without fearing their errors. As the students become more comfortable with the material, Amanda increases the points awarded for correct answers. Together we all strive to help our students become learners who are adept at justifying their thinking. We try to model shared inquiry by creating a culture that focuses on effort and progress rather than recrimination.

We believe learning should extend beyond the confines of our classrooms. This does not give us permission to take end-of-year field trips to amusement parks or visit museums without adequately preparing students for what they will see there. Outside activities can provide crucial curriculum connections and should never be considered "free" days or unstructured child care. Young adolescents need opportunities to see learning in action, to understand that their education has a purpose. We stress service-learning projects that enable students to work with professionals in the community, seek solutions to real social and political problems, and apply their developing skills in literacy, mathematics, science, history, and technology.

We believe that students must be actively engaged in learning so they will take ownership of their education and pride in class activities. Our students rarely sit in their desks filling out worksheets. Our lessons provide opportunities for students to meet standards as they move around, gather data, make decisions, and solve problems. On a daily basis our students are engaged in activities such as blowing bubbles in the parking lot before writing figurative language, waltzing around the classroom during a reading of Poe's "Masque of the Red Death," participating in a scavenger hunt to locate geometric concepts in commonplace objects, and simulating wildlife population data sampling using Goldfish crackers. There is a constant buzz of activity in our classrooms as students meet the required curriculum standards through innovative and engaging activities.

We believe that families are essential partners. When our students leave school, they might not mention the day's events to their families. Young adolescents are notoriously tight-lipped about their activities. Yet families need to know what's going on so they can support their children's education. By creating partnerships with families, we help improve the dialogue. For example, after we'd read the Gettysburg Address in class and listened to the soundtrack of the movie *Gettysburg*, Greg's grandmother contacted us through email. She asked us how to find the music. "Greg said it was very relaxing and he enjoyed it," she wrote. "And I'm all for anything that will encourage music appreciation. So many children only know rap and hip hop. It would be wonderful to enrich his life with something classical. I guess you better not mention that I emailed you. It would probably embarrass him." It's our job to encourage participation from families by keeping them informed of class activities so that they can enjoy and support their children's educational experiences.

We believe that teachers should learn along with their students. We are not almighty givers of knowledge. We are also knowledge seekers. We ask students to help us discover and interpret information so they can see that learning is a reciprocal process. For instance, when Monique was asked to serve on a reading committee, she was expected to discuss literacy strategies that were most advantageous to middle school students. Monique had a clear picture of what she thought were the most successful strategies, but she realized she was missing our students' perspective. So she asked for their input. They reminded her that being able to choose their reading material was the strongest inducement to read. Monique had left this strategy off the list initially because she didn't think it was pedagogically important. However, as a student named Denzel pointed out, "If we won't read, it doesn't matter which strategy you try to teach us. Picking books makes us want to read. You have to include it."

Finally, we believe that learning is a lifelong endeavor, and we are absolutely certain that every student can make a positive difference in the world. We encourage our students to begin influencing our community while they are still members of our team. To combat illiteracy, which is a significant problem in Louisiana, our students developed an interdisciplinary project, "For the Love of Literacy." They wrote hundreds of letters inviting schools to participate and spent the year maintaining a website (http://teacherweb.com/la/dutchtownmiddleschool/fortheloveofliteracy) that featured their choices of great literature. They hosted community book talks, communicated via the Internet with students and authors, created literacy posters to distribute throughout the country, appeared in commercials promoting literacy, visited local book stores to assist customers in selecting good books, read books aloud to children in the Head Start program, guided book discussions for our school's fifth graders, collected books to distribute to Hurricane Katrina survivors, and filled a library at an urban community center. We confidently hand over the reins of such projects to our students so they realize they can contribute positively to society.

Open for Discussion

Coming to these core beliefs requires sufficient time, reflection, and honest dialogue among team members. The best conversations sometimes sneak up on us.

"What do you do when a child doesn't have a pencil?"

This may not seem to be a very pressing concern, but it was the first question asked during our initial team meeting of the 2006–2007 school year. Erin Babin was new to our group, and this issue was on her mind.

"Give them one," we replied.

"Really?" Erin asked, still skeptical. "Aren't they responsible for bringing their own supplies? I mean, last year I could have gone through a box of pencils a day."

What we quickly realized was that Erin's question involved more than establishing common procedures for the team. It required a deeper discussion about our philosophy of learning. To reach a consensus, we had to revisit our core beliefs and see how this seemingly simple procedure fit within the context of our team goals.

If we truly believed as a team that "school should be an equitable place where all students have opportunities to succeed," then a student without a pencil would not be able to fairly compete. Of course, we also want to stress personal responsibility, a key skill for young adolescents. So we chose a team policy that seemed to strike a balance between those two objectives.

We decided to buy extra pencils for our classrooms. To manage the supplies, we adopted the "shoe method" used by another teacher at our school. This approach involves exchanging a shoe for a pencil. A student borrows a pencil, and we keep his or her shoe (or some other item that students value) as collateral. At the end of class, the pencil and shoe are returned to their rightful owners. By adopting this method, we solved the pencil problem and created a consistent team procedure that matched our core beliefs as educators. Although teams can exist without shared educational philosophies, they flourish when team members can agree about the most effective ways to teach young adolescents. Otherwise, small disagreements, such as what to do when a child doesn't have a pencil, can distract from the more important work of building team unity and students' success.

This is not to say that teams must be made up of people with the same personalities. Different styles can be healthy, as long as team members support a mutual mission. Our former team member Larry Chambless used to joke that Monique and Amanda were hot-air balloons floating from one idea to the next and he was the rope that kept them grounded. Because of our distinctive personalities, this was an apt analogy for how our team worked. Larry's down-to-earth approach reminded us to consider the practicalities of any new scheme. On the flip side, Larry became more daring and imaginative as he joined us on some spectacular thrill rides. Our willingness to celebrate each person's individuality and make light of each other's quirks stemmed from our respect for shared team values.

Effective interdisciplinary teams ensure that every member makes important contributions. Some teachers, like Amanda, are the dreamers who continually conjure imaginative ideas to engage students and integrate the curriculum. Some teachers, like Monique, are the natural enforcers who delegate responsibilities and ensure that necessary follow-through occurs. Other teachers are like Kathryn. They have great organizational skills, which keep the team humming, but they also focus on "heart" issues, reminding everyone to keep students' needs and interests at the center of all decisions. Truly effective teams perform like highly skilled orchestras, creating harmony while enabling individual musicians to make distinctive sounds. The beauty of working together is that you don't have to be good at everything. Each teacher does not need to create, enforce, and organize simultaneously. On a team, you can play to your strengths while sharing the load. There are opportunities for everyone to work diligently at doing what comes naturally.

A case in point: In April 2007, Kathryn got married and left us for a week while on her honeymoon. During her absence, the school had an early dismissal, which required us to use an alternate class schedule. In the past, any changes would have been marked on our team whiteboards first thing in the morning. However, on this particular day, Kathryn wasn't there to handle this vital but overlooked task. Amanda and Monique spent an hour and sent fifteen emails to the office trying to obtain the appropriate schedule. Of course, all of us had received copies of the alternative schedule at the beginning of the school year. But, truth be told, we had never had to look at the information because one of Kathryn's roles on our team is keeping up with administrative correspondence. We never realized before what a luxury it was to have teammates who managed the minutiae for us. What freedom! We'll never take that responsibility for granted again.

Lightening the Load

Relinquishing control of every duty was frightening when we initially established an instructional team. However, once we became accustomed to relying on others to contribute for the team's benefit, we understood the value of sharing. Most importantly, we have more time and capacity to address students' needs because we don't feel burned out.

National trends indicate that 35 to 50 percent of new teachers leave the profession within the first three years (National Commission on Teaching and

America's Future 2003). Many new teachers cite lack of support from school leadership, weak organizational structures, and disrespectful work conditions as their chief reasons for quitting (Ingersoll 2001; Johnson, Birkeland, Kardos, Kauffman, Liu, and Peske 2001).

When we ask fellow teachers to identify the major sources of their frustrations, few mention students. For many, other issues cause significant stress. Seemingly simple tasks can accumulate so rapidly that an individual teacher quickly becomes overwhelmed. Teams can offer support, such as reducing the clerical issues that clog a teacher's day. On our team, Kathryn takes care of all the letters sent home to notify parents of students' poor attendance. Why should all of us be responsible for this task when Kathryn can do it efficiently and effectively? On the other hand, why should Kathryn or Amanda have to understand every technological innovation when Monique enjoys learning about hardware, software, and gadgets? If we worked in isolation, we would have to perform every job ourselves, duplicating each effort three times!

Teaming enables us to explore the instructional ideas we couldn't advance when we juggled so many other responsibilities alone. Erin Babin described the possibilities in this way: "Because of teaming, I have become more knowledgeable, more motivated, and more apt to take risks. This has led to the implementation of new teaching techniques that I never would have tried before. I have successfully integrated reading strategies within the context of science, and I have seen students make connections across the curriculum that neither they nor I could have made before I was part of a team."

Consider what Kathryn accomplished by becoming part of a multidisciplinary group. During spring break in her first year of teaching, the school principal, Mr. Walker, asked Kathryn to join our eighth-grade team for the last nine weeks of school. Our school district was investigating various special education inclusion models for the following year. Walker wanted to test the waters for a team-teaching model that included a special education teacher working alongside the core subject teachers. Up to that time, Kathryn had been responsible for teaching five self-contained remedial language arts classes. Although Kathryn was excited about collaborating with other teachers and including her special education students in a regular classroom setting, she was nervous about entering an established team well into the school year. When the principal said he wanted her to spend forty-five minutes every afternoon specifically helping Amanda "address the needs of such a wide variety of academic levels" in math, Kathryn had no idea how challenging the assignment would be. But thanks to Kathryn's interventions, Amanda would soon discover why so many struggling students were falling through the cracks.

That first day in Amanda's math class, the algebra lesson focused on multiplying variables and whole numbers and combining like terms, such as (x + 2) (x – 3). The students were following a commonly used strategy known as FOIL (multiply the First terms, multiply the Outer terms, multiply the Inner terms, multiply the Last terms, then combine like terms). Most students quickly caught on to the formula and solved the problems with ease. However, some students couldn't grasp the concept no matter how many examples Amanda showed them; they continued multiplying the wrong terms. At first, Kathryn couldn't understand how something so logical and sequential could stymie the students. That is, until a student cried out in frustration, "I just don't see it!"

As Kathryn looked up at the whiteboard to point to one of the numerous examples, the difficulty dawned on her. "How *could* he *see* it," she thought to herself. "The whiteboard was filled with problems all written in black marker."

Although Amanda was in the midst of direct instruction, Kathryn walked from the back of the classroom to the front, took four colored markers, and began drawing arrows connecting each step in the problem in a different color. Amanda cocked her head to the side so she could see what Kathryn was doing, then returned to the lesson without saying a word. By the next day, every student in the class understood how to multiply variables, not because they had been shown a better way, but a different way.

It was an eye-opening experience for everyone to see how Amanda trusted a novice teacher to weave instruction into her own lesson and how Kathryn confidently provided an alternate method of solving problems in a veteran teacher's classroom. This might seem like a small incident, but it had huge implications for two strangers who were learning to work together on an expanding team. Amanda and Kathryn realized the benefits of including a special education teacher in the mainstream core class. Not only were they able to complement one another's teaching techniques, they were able to meet the needs of all the students in the class.

Growing Pains

It's essential to review goals and beliefs each time a new team is formed, even if several members have worked together before. Misunderstandings will still occur, but circling back to your common agenda can reduce the friction. For example, although Monique and Amanda had taught together for several years, Kathryn's presence caused us to reconsider, renegotiate, and revise.

The same was true when Katie Sheffield moved onto our team fresh out of college. Katie was excited about getting the job in January, halfway through the school year. She spent a large portion of her December holiday preparing the classroom to which she'd been assigned. Katie cleaned out closets, redecorated, and created marvelous lesson plans to greet her students.

When we returned from the holiday break, Katie's first day went smoothly. There were no problems until lunch, when Monique frantically searched through the file cabinet in Katie's classroom to find a paper plate and utensils.

"Who moved our paper plates?" Monique demanded.

"What do you mean *our* paper plates?" Katie asked with a bewildered look on her face. "I thought those just belonged to the person who was in here before me. Why would they belong to everyone? I'll get some more plates. I'll get some more forks, too. I threw those away with the plates while I was cleaning."

What Katie had not realized was that our team shares everything. All of our supplies are located in certain areas of our team space. It is not uncommon for Amanda to walk into Monique's room to retrieve loose-leaf paper or for Kathryn to enter Amanda's room to get markers. What Monique had forgotten was that Katie had not been privy to all of the team-building activities during which we had established our operating system. So, midyear, we had to revisit these procedures so Katie could assimilate.

The paper plate caper led to a minor conflict, which we immediately laughed about once Monique's hunger pangs subsided. However, other issues can spiral out of control when team cohesiveness is lacking.

Though we could easily laugh off the incident with Katie, not all transitions with new team members have gone so smoothly. In another year, one of our principals asked us to interview potential candidates for open spots on our team. This courtesy was extended in an effort to avoid problems that might develop because of incompatible combinations. Because we needed a new partner, we assisted our principal in selecting a teacher whom we thought would be a perfect addition to our team. Creating our team identity was a positive experience, and we were hopeful for the future.

During the first quarter everything seemed fine. By the end of the second quarter, however, we were ready to scream. Our new partner did not follow through on any team decisions. In fact, this teacher ignored or undermined many of the decisions we'd collectively agreed to support and told students not to tell us about the inconsistencies.

We silently suffered until the December holiday. Then, after we discussed and purchased the gifts we would give to the students as a team, our teaching partner purchased and distributed "especially from me" gifts instead. This forced us into action! At our next team meeting, we finally confronted this teacher. We articulated why we thought the individual gesture would undermine the team concept we had developed. As it turned out, our teammate was unaware that the gift would make us feel slighted. Furthermore, this partner was oblivious to how other actions had prompted our animosity and stress. Openly discussing our concerns actually helped us solve many of the problems we were experiencing on the team. It wasn't an easy process, but it was essential to our later success.

Sometimes professional confrontation is necessary to prime team communications and develop more focused goals. Conflict management skills are essential to team unity. Let's face it: we can't simply get new team members when problems arise. We are part of the team for the duration. Conflicts provide us an opportunity to practice what we preach to our students when they are involved in disputes. This is quite difficult in the midst of heated discussions, so it is essential to maintain focus on the problem at hand and the task that must be addressed rather than falling into the temptation of making personal attacks.

For six years, two of us—Monique and Amanda—had worked together on a team without having a serious argument. The two of us often disagreed about lessons and procedural issues, but we had never openly challenged each other's fundamental beliefs about working in the best interest of students. After discovering that one of our students was to be expelled, however, we both became extremely emotional. Amanda thought we should do more to help the student. Monique thought the boy was his own worst enemy and needed to face the consequences of his actions. After an intense debate, we ran out of steam and started to really listen to each other's perspective. Amanda realized that we might not be capable of saving every student. Monique acknowledged that, for the first time, she did not have the desire to try. These insights were not easy for either of us to accept. During the argument, we raised our voices in anger and spoke words that did not carry our true intent. In the end, we were actually on the same side of the issue, but we had been too emotional to recognize it from the start.

When passionate people work together, emotions are bound to overflow at times. What keeps them from becoming hostile is working through conflict. After taking time to cool off overnight, we reassembled at the next team meeting to establish a set of guidelines for helping the student who was on the verge of expulsion. Monique agreed with Amanda that we should present the positive aspects of the boy's school experiences when we met with the district review board, in the hope of giving him one more chance. Amanda agreed with Monique that we would preface our plea for another chance with clear communications to the student and his parents that this was our last attempt to intervene. From this point forward, whenever the student made a poor choice, he would suffer the full consequences of his actions, as specified by school policy.

Conflict is not only inevitable; it is a normal stage in team formation and development. Sylvia Roberts and Eunice Pruitt (2003) identify the various stages of team formation in their book, *Schools as Professional Learning Communities*. The five stages of team building are as follows:

1. Forming: Team members become a unified group.
2. Storming: Turmoil interferes with productivity as team members learn their functions on the team.
3. Norming: A time of reduced conflict and greater collegiality ensues.
4. Performing: This is the most productive stage, in which there is clear understanding of goals, desired outcomes, and team members' roles.
5. Adjourning: The team disperses, sometimes as a result of faculty changes, school growth, promotions, and so on.

Our team has navigated through each of the stages, and now we consistently operate at the performing level. One of the reasons we can work at the upper ranges of Roberts and Pruitt's scale is because all of us follow the same established procedures. As a result, we no longer have to spend so much time thinking about them. They are habitual, which frees us to shift our attention to integrating instruction rather than continually dealing with discipline issues caused by students who are confused about what to do. That way, the only surprises for students come during fun educational activities.

Establishing Team Classroom Procedures

The following questions address procedural issues we have found helpful to address before the school year begins. Some represent major undertakings, and some are minor; but all contribute to the seamless flow of instruction and learning.

Discipline

- What are the rules that will be enforced in every classroom on the team?
- What protocol will you use for giving warnings about behavior, contacting parents, and writing conduct infractions or referrals?

Grading

- What are the guidelines for grading written work?
- What are the guidelines for accepting late work?
- When and how will completed assignments be returned to students?
- How will parents be informed of their children's progress?
- What procedures will be followed when students want to take home portfolios of their work to share with their families?

Bonus Opportunities

- Will bonus points be allowed on tests and major projects? What about extra-credit assignments?

Parent Conferences

- Will you always meet as a team with parents, regardless of how well a student is performing in a particular class?
- Who will contact parents to remind them of conferences? What communication methods will they use?
- How will you communicate unpleasant information to families? What style or method of delivery will you use?

Bathroom Visits

- How often will students be allowed to visit the restroom during a class period or school day?
- What are the appropriate times?
- Who will take students to the restroom as part of the daily routine?

Homework and Tests

- How much homework will be assigned each night?
- How many tests are allowable on a given day?
- What procedures will be used to grade homework?
- How will parents be notified of missed homework assignments?
- How will make-up work be handled?

Student Supplies

- How will you store supplies and replace missing supplies?

Headings for Papers

- (*Seems silly, but this one is really important to students!*) How will students title their work, and where will they place their names and dates on assignments?

Before teaming, we had to reteach our individual classroom routines on a nearly daily basis. With a traditional class schedule, our students had to contend with seven different teachers, each of whom wanted things done her way during the day: a recipe for confusion. Teamwork enabled us to develop consistency so our students could follow the same procedures throughout the day. They no longer had to wonder how Mrs. Mayeaux wanted them to put a heading on their papers or whether Mrs. Wild expected them to turn in their homework assignments each morning. The procedures are standard across the entire team.

Daily Team Planning Periods

Establishing common procedures does not guarantee automatic acceptance or success on a team. Putting plans into action takes practice and vigilance. During our first months together, we met periodically throughout the summer and thought we had created the dream team. Then school began, and reality set in. We did not have the luxury of sipping coffee at Monique's house as we planned strategies. We were surrounded by squirrelly students and bombarded with our jobs' escalating requirements. Fortunately, our principal had allocated fifty minutes a day for team planning, in addition to our personal planning periods. Then and now, this schedule is one of the main reasons we were able to learn how to function effectively.

Some administrators are hesitant to give teachers more time "off" during the school day, but this is a mistake. When used appropriately, common team planning periods serve a vital role in interdisciplinary instruction, provide a reliable structure for professional growth, and lead to gains in student achievement. Moreover, teams that meet frequently are happier and more productive in their work (Flowers, Mertens, and Mulhall 1999). Despite research and experience that have demonstrated these benefits, a recent national survey found that only 59 percent of middle school teams have both common and individual planning periods (Hackmann et al. 2002).

Recently, at a literacy meeting conducted by our state department of education, the presenter stressed the importance of maximizing instructional time. He stated that teachers should be teaching at least 90 percent of the school day and administrators should not allow time to be wasted on "off" periods. Amanda asked about team planning and embedded professional development. The presenter scoffed, saying he had never seen teachers use such time effectively.

Unfortunately, many administrators feel the same way. We counter that misconception by following the old adage, "What gets checked, gets done." We have found that teaming time is most effective when administrators do the following:

1. Require teams to maintain a team binder with documentation of each day's meeting notes

2. Check the team binder at least quarterly to see what's been happening

3. Pop in to team meetings to listen, observe, and show interest

4. Schedule time at least biweekly to meet with the team or a group of teams for a pulse check

5. Schedule time before the new school year to meet with teams and explain expectations

Because team meetings can easily deteriorate into unproductive fussing fits and gripe sessions, we have established strict procedures for our gatherings. We want to maximize our time together and maintain our focus on student achievement. Figure 1.1 provides a sample framework.

We include these major categories in our weekly agenda because we must address them if we want our team to operate smoothly. However, our agendas are not limited to the items listed. By setting time limits for each topic, we are able to quickly address managerial issues and then move on to more complex instructional concerns.

Weekly Team Meeting Agenda	
Monday	· Overview of the week's agenda · Plan daily agenda for the week · Long-term planning for curriculum integration
Tuesday	· Conferences with parents (if scheduled) · Concerns/adjustments/new ideas regarding inclusion of special needs students
Wednesday	· School Building Level Committee to review student services and evaluations, individualized education plan reviews, and 504 plan reviews (Are students' special needs/modifications being met, and are their goals being addressed?) · Conferences with parents (if scheduled)
Thursday	· Meet with administrators if needed to discuss upcoming team/school events · Weekly grade-level meeting with teacher coach for professional development (topics may include analyzing student work, developing classroom strategies, discussing educational articles, and new technology inservices)
Friday	· Review anecdotal notes about students' academic performance and any behavior/discipline issues · Develop list of parents we need to contact for support · Preview instructional plans for the following week and discuss any upcoming tests, class projects, special events, etc.

Figure 1.1 Sample Weekly Team Meeting Agenda

Special education students' needs often figure into the conversation. We use our team meetings to monitor our instructional modifications and review students' academic progress. When we see some gaps, we ask the school's instructional coach to visit and help us identify some research-based strategies that could help. For example, when our special education students were having trouble taking notes from multiple sources, our coach provided us with information about using graphic organizers and other helpful techniques.

In addition to a weekly schedule, daily agendas can sharpen a team's focus and enable members to document their progress. We suggest creating an agenda with a specific time limit for each topic. This encourages constructive dialogue and keeps the conversation flowing. We agree that if an issue has not been resolved by the end of the allotted time, we will bring it up for discussion in the future. Then we move on to the next topic on the agenda.

We keep our agendas in a team binder, and each of us adds to the lists as needed. This way, we don't forget important issues but we also don't interrupt instruction to discuss items that are better saved for team meetings.

We are mindful of how time-consuming and complicated it can be for administrators to arrange common planning periods for teams, so we strive to use our time well. We also provide regular updates to the principal to demonstrate the benefits of having a team planning period. Figure 1.2 suggests one possible framework for reporting information about the team's activities.

The range of items on the agenda varies considerably and can include curriculum, classroom management, and state standards, among others. For example, we might discuss current staff development

Daily Team Meeting Agenda

Asteroid Team Daily Agenda			
Date: _____			

Team Members Present: _____Monique Wild _____Amanda Mayeaux _____Kathryn Edmonds		Others in Attendance:	
Agenda Item	Time Allotted	Notes	Resolution or Action Plan/ Who's Responsible?

Figure 1.2 Sample Daily Team Meeting Agenda

opportunities available in the school district or research outside options. We might review our plans for parent conferences or develop a response to a recent family powwow. Other recurring topics include multidisciplinary connections, service-learning activities, and common student behavior problems. Although we try to prevent discipline disturbances by setting standard team procedures and explaining our expectations from the first day, we can't always keep the ship on a steady course. Sometimes the turbulence seems to be bad behavior but actually stems from a faulty procedure.

"Goodness, I am so tired of dealing with cafeteria issues," Amanda said one day during our common planning period. "I mean, every single day our team is pointed out for doing ridiculous stuff like hitting and pinching. I may scream."

"Yeah, I have had it, too," Monique agreed. "But I hate punishing everyone because it really is just a few kids doing silly things."

"So, what can we do?" Amanda asked.

Kathryn cut to the chase. "Well, I think one of the issues is we are rotating cafeteria duty each day, so no one knows what happened the day before. The kids are using this to their advantage."

Monique suggested that we start looking for misbehavior patterns, and Amanda offered to create a checklist that each teacher could use to collect and report infractions.

"So then what?" Kathryn asked, once again focusing on results.

"We need to come up with a standard punishment for misbehaving," said Monique. "I think if they have three marks, we call home."

"I like it," Kathryn agreed.

Amanda also assented and offered to explain the procedures and consequences to our students, which led to consistency across the team and a decrease in cafeteria discipline problems.

Although the previous example reflects a conversation about procedures, the majority of our team meetings revolve around what's working—or not working—in our classrooms.

"I am so excited," Monique said during another team meeting. "The kids really got into the discussion today about [the short story] 'Desiree's Baby.' It was one of the best share circles we have had, ever."

"Did you do something differently this time?" asked Amanda.

"Yes, I decided to use a reading guide like the one I saw Roger Farr present [at a conference] in Portland. This story is really difficult, but the reading guide allowed everyone to have access to the discussion. I also made them talk in small groups first. Each group brought three things to talk about in the share circle."

"I think I would like to try something like that in my math discussions next week," Amanda said, and the conversation turned to how we could incorporate this teaching method into other classes.

These rich conversations, one of the direct benefits of common team planning periods, have spurred us to think and grow professionally. We laugh as we recall the first year when a simple issue such as cafeteria behavior problems would have taken the whole session to solve. We have become more efficient through practice at finding answers because, frankly, we would rather spend the time discussing students' learning.

ChapterTwo
Show Them How Much You Care

The students applauded and high-fived as LaToya slowly returned to her seat following her science presentation. A casual observer might have been perplexed, for there was nothing special about LaToya's performance. She stood in front of the classroom, barely made eye contact with her teachers and peers, and spoke so quietly that it was hard to hear the perfunctory information she presented. Then she sat. So why did her classmates spontaneously rise to their feet and cheer? Because LaToya had never spoken publicly to our team before that day.

At the beginning of the school year, LaToya did not make eye contact with anyone. When we called on her during class activities, she was completely nonresponsive. She rarely took out books or attempted her assignments. She did not join small- or large-group activities. She remained at her seat, staring at the top of her desk. At recess, she stood against the wall and looked at the ground. She did not have any friends nor did she seem to take interest in any part of her education.

As her teachers, of course, we did what we could to make connections with LaToya. We stood near her to build intimacy, talked to her, joked with her, assisted her with her assignments, and shared our dreams for her success. By the second week of school, however, we knew we needed a deeper understanding of LaToya's situation than we could uncover in her academic records. Kathryn contacted her mother and set up a conference. We discovered that LaToya's condition stemmed from an illness and that the medication she took caused her to withdraw. Years before, she had been as talkative as any other child.

We assured LaToya's mother that we had her daughter's best interests in mind, and we discussed possible action plans to assist LaToya socially and academically. We all left the conference with a common goal to help LaToya interact with others so that she might begin to achieve academically. In the end, however, it was our students who were most responsible for LaToya's transformation.

Austin was the first classmate to reach out to her. He volunteered to help LaToya with her assignments, asked to sit by her in class, and made a point to talk to her during lunch and recess. Other students followed Austin's lead and began asking LaToya questions that only required a yes or no answer. When she failed to respond, they created a system of comments and cues:

"If you want to join us, give me five."

"If you like my new haircut, smile."

When LaToya wasn't interested in interacting, they would simply rattle on about their adolescent lives as though she really had answered their questions.

"I know what you're thinking; you're thinking that I should let my hair grow."

Eventually, LaToya stopped attempting to remove herself from these one-way conversations, but she never initiated them.

One day the principal was watching LaToya on the playground during recess. He noticed that as LaToya leaned against the school building, she was silently observing the other students instead of staring at the ground. This stunned the principal. He had been observing LaToya for years and had never seen her show any interest in her peers. He also noted that LaToya had begun smiling and making eye contact whenever people greeted her. The principal encouraged us to continue whatever we were doing to help LaToya emerge from her shell.

During the next few months, LaToya made progress in excruciatingly small increments. She completed a few math problems, read part of a book, took some notes, smiled when someone said hello, and stepped away from the wall at recess to stand among the children who were throwing balls. LaToya's classmates and teachers noted these improvements and celebrated each one.

Then big things started to happen. Our language arts curriculum required students to write poetry using various forms and techniques and to publish their poems using technology. To provide an authentic purpose for writing, Monique invited students to make their families the intended audience of their poems. Valentine's Day was coming up, so she asked students to create PowerPoint presentations they would send home to their parents via email. On the day we taped voice-over messages to greet parents when they opened their email messages, LaToya stood and walked to the recorder with minimal prompting. Though she did not speak, she made the trip to the recorder three times. On the third attempt, she smiled while standing at the microphone.

Later that month, during a small-group discussion in language arts class, Austin asked LaToya to read a paragraph, and she did—every word—as naturally and spontaneously as if she responded this way every day. LaToya's classmates congratulated her, Monique feigned a fainting spell brought on by extreme pride, Kathryn squealed with delight, and LaToya beamed.

Then, on the day scheduled for the science presentation, LaToya really broke through her reserve. Her classmates and teachers expected her to smile, make partial eye contact, and sit down. But to our delight, LaToya did much more, and her efforts earned her superstar status on the team. The students understood how far she had come, so LaToya's accomplishments felt like their own. Our typically self-absorbed middle school students had made LaToya part of our team.

"Don't Be Hatin' on Me!"

LaToya's story illustrates the significant achievements that are possible when teaching teams develop strong, positive relationships with students, parents, and administrators and set standards for behavior that go beyond "thou shalt not" rules. High-functioning teams are concerned about building up, not tearing down. They focus on belonging, making sure that all students—not just the easy ones—are valued and respected. When teams establish these bonds, they become an extended family whose members work together to ensure mutual success. Brittany, one of our students, shows how young adolescents take this message to heart: "Not only do you have to put forth your best effort, but you must walk into class with a great smile and tell each other that you love each other every day. That is what our team is all about."

Our students have proven time and again that young adolescents are capable of demonstrating compassionate and loving concern for others. Middle school students are more than just "hormones on legs," as one of our friends, a kindergarten teacher, jokingly refers to them. While some view young adolescents as miniadults and others see them as overgrown, hairy children, effective middle school teachers know that their students are unique. Middle school students are exuberant, erratic, exhausting, and entertaining—and this is what makes middle school teaching so challenging and so rewarding.

Middle school students are struggling to become independent of authority, yet they constantly seek approval from others. Among the developmental needs of middle school students identified by Scales (1991) are meaningful school experiences, positive social interactions with adults and peers, and community involvement activities that enable them to define themselves. Interdisciplinary teams give young adolescents a comfortable place to try on new roles while providing supports that will enable them to maintain positive relationships, create an identity with a school community, learn how to accept responsibility for their actions, and contribute to their own educational experiences.

To teach middle school students effectively, educators must build rapport with them. We have repeatedly discovered that success with young adolescents stems from trust. When the relationships are genuine, students will do whatever is expected of them and are most willing to please. However, if students consider the relationships to be contrived or superficial, they will employ the most creative methods to undermine classroom activities. Quite simply, our students must know that we genuinely care about them.

"Building teacher-student relationships is, in fact, so important that it is arguably the most important factor contributing to the success of students, both behaviorally and academically. Students who experience respect and unconditional acceptance from their teacher are more likely to be compliant, respectful, and open to learning" (Dahlgren 2005, 103).

Although Madeline Hunter may have summarized these crucial connections most eloquently—"Kids don't care how much you know until they know how much you care" (Dahlgren 2005, 111)—a student named Markeith gave them authenticity every time he yelled out, "Don't be hatin' on me." This admonition, uttered whenever Markeith noticed that we were becoming frustrated, caused us to step back and examine our behaviors and practices. "Don't be hatin' on me" became a team mantra that reminded us how much our attitudes affect students' ability to learn.

"The truth is that you may not 'like' a student or 'love' a student, but as educators who are entrusted with learners in our charge we must learn to care for and accept students for their inherent value," author and educator Rick Dahlgren (2005, 113) reminds us.

Let's face it, some days it is extremely difficult to love all students. But we never stop trying. Markeith voiced the young adolescent's continual search for validation. Middle school students want to know that their teachers care enough to challenge them intellectually, reprimand them when they misbehave, and praise them when they demonstrate progress.

Even after moving to high school, Markeith and LaToya would pop into our classrooms to visit, usually when they were struggling to adapt to their new surroundings. Like newly trained pilots, middle school students are eager to fly solo as long as they can circle back to base when they need to refuel and confirm their destinations.

"We need a good fussin,' Mrs. Mayeaux," Markeith told Amanda one afternoon during his ninth-grade year.

All students want to know that they are worthy of our time, energy, and high expectations. When team members work together to reinforce this message, students should never feel that their teachers are hatin' on them.

Welcome to the Team

To build positive relationships with our students, we try to become part of their lives before they enter our classrooms. We open the lines of communication when our future students least expect it, during the summer. Sometimes we send postcards from our vacation sites or "Welcome to the Team" flyers and include our email addresses and website. Some years we actually receive return postcards from our future students. For example, Dylan wrote to tell us about his summer travels and offered recommendations about sites to see during the field trip to the nation's capital that we had foreshadowed in our welcoming postcards. By the time students arrive to start the fall term, they are full of anticipation about our team.

The first order of business when the new school year begins is to find out as much as possible about our students. We distribute interest inventories that ask for students' perceptions about school and different subject areas and information about their personal and educational backgrounds. At our first team meeting during the school year, we review these surveys and note interesting facts about each student. We learned that LaToya hadn't spoken aloud in a few years, that Regan loved to dance, and that Austin was a skateboard fanatic. During the first week of school, we make a point of referencing this data in conversations and classroom activities. Monique told Austin about a skateboard competition that would be shown on a cable television channel over the weekend. Kathryn mentioned that she would be attending every football game and keeping an eye on David, whose size made him a natural star on the team. Amanda mentioned to Justin that she had seen his father at Wal-Mart the night before. Through these exchanges, students begin to understand that our interest in them extends beyond the classroom.

In addition to surveys, we use dialogue journals to communicate with our students about a multitude of topics. Nancie Atwell (1998) pioneered this strategy for conducting authentic conversations in her middle school literature and language arts classes, in which she sought to simulate a dining room or drawing room discussion. In reflecting upon the noneducational conversations about literature that she'd had with avid readers, Atwell found that there was an informal air about them akin to discussing a movie after leaving the theater. Atwell's book *In the Middle* reveals several ways she incorporated simulated kitchen-table conversations into her students' learning experiences—both in oral and written discussions.

We have adapted the journal approach she describes and have extended it to include students' families and school administrators. For example, our students write to their parents and point to evidence of their academic progress reflected in their portfolios. When working with students, we have three nonnegotiable rules for dialogue journals:

1. Students must write a full page of reflection, which encourages them to dig deeply into the topic presented.
2. Students must write to the assigned person. This may include one of their teachers, administrators, fellow students, or their families.
3. Journals are always answered promptly, most often within twenty-four hours so that students receive immediate feedback.

Although we use dialogue journals throughout the school year to check for understanding or challenge students to consider different interpretations, the goal of our initial communications is relationship building. We ask questions such as the following:

- What do you expect to learn this school year?
- What have you heard about our team that you want to know about?
- What do we need to know about you so that we can teach you effectively?

Dialogue journal topics addressing academic areas often focus on helping students make connections across the curriculum:

- In Mrs. Wild's room there is a banner with a quote by Margaret Meade: "Never doubt that a small group of thoughtful, committed citizens can change the world. Indeed, it is the only thing that ever has." What does the quote mean to you? How does it relate to what we are learning? How does this quote relate to our team?

- It is ironic that Gregory Johnson (of *Texas v. Johnson*) was arrested for burning the American flag when the proper procedure for disposing of the flag, according to many sources, is to burn it. Explain how tone and symbolism played an important part in this case. Do you think Johnson had the right to burn the flag? Why, or why not?

Some journal topics are more reflective in nature: Describe your reading habits. How have they changed since the beginning of the school year? What do you notice about your reading habits? What caused you to change your habits or keep them the same?

Initially, Monique was the only one of us who used dialogue journals, and she did so to discuss literature, as described in Atwell's book. However, the rest of us quickly saw the benefits of using dialogue journals to reinforce teaming. Each time students write in dialogue journals we gain valuable information about who they are, what they know, what they require of us, and how we should plan instruction. Using dialogue journals as a team tool has enabled all of us to be part of the students' writing audience, regardless of the class period or subject matter in which the journal was assigned. The journals provide us with a clearer picture of the total student, and our students are able to see that we value learning in all disciplines. Monique uses dialogue journals to discuss science topics, Amanda shares information about interesting books, and Kathryn suggests better methods of solving math problems. In addition, because we share the responsibility of responding to the dialogue journals, we have time to offer more substantive feedback. Instead of having to write back to ninety students individually, we can respond to thirty each. The lightened load helps us reflect on our students' progress and design appropriate interventions instead of feeling burdened and eager to get done.

The morning after they have turned in their journal assignments, students can expect to find their notebooks with our detailed comments inside. They eagerly open the notebooks to find out what we have written in response to their entries. The cumulative written communications documented in our team dialogue journals serve as a reflective record of our discussions and our learning together throughout the school year.

Periodically our students address their journal entries to their parents. This helps strengthen home/school connections and can be an effective way of closing the communication gap between students and parents that tends to widen in middle school. Consider the following correspondence between Sarah and her mother:

Dear Mom,

I really enjoy being on the Flying Pigs team. I love all of my teachers. I think I'm really improving this year. I like doing the Love of Literacy Campaign and the Online Learning Café.

This year I'm reading more books than I've ever read. Since this summer I've read 25 books. It's a good thing Mrs. Wild has a huge library because I would run out of books if she didn't.

I think we both agree that I need to get to school on time. Let's leave the house by 6:45 every morning. I need help on one-step equations, but last time I asked you to help with equations, I ended up crying. Let's try again!

Love,
Sarah

Dear Sarah,

I am so proud of your accomplishments. You are a wonderful student. I think it is awesome that you love to read and learn.

I would love to help you with equations if you are willing to listen and not just say, "I don't understand." I hope that you listen before you decide if you understand. Don't give up on it!

I think your greatest accomplishment is who you are. . . . You are compassionate and fun loving . . . and you have a great sense of humor.

Keep it up!

I love you,
Mom

Journals are not the only written form of communication we use to build relationships with students. Like all teachers, we have students who enter our classrooms with notorious reputations. We make it a point to catch these students doing something good during the first week of school, when most are on their best behavior. As soon as we spot the superlatives, we write the first of our "love notes" and send them home. When Amanda wrote a love note praising Sean's leadership abilities, he was shocked and proud. His sense of accomplishment sustained him as he sought to live up to Amanda's assessment of his abilities. Throughout the year he used his leadership skills positively rather than disruptively. When he slipped, we only had to remind him of the first love note that Amanda had placed in his agenda planner, and his demeanor changed.

Sharing an Identity

Love notes don't resonate with every student, so we enlist all of the students' support in creating our team's identity and goals. Trusting your students to shape the team that you have worked so hard to develop is not easy. But without a real role in the team's formation or a sense of ownership, students won't respect the values their teachers want to share; nor will students feel that they belong to a family unit, which is our ultimate goal.

At the beginning of the school year, our students create their team name and motto, decorate the classrooms based on their chosen themes, and share their strengths and weaknesses in order to establish an effective organization of peer tutors. These are welcome changes for students who typically enter a classroom where the themes have been determined, all wall space has been covered with teacher-selected decor, and the peer groups already have been arranged.

Before our students decide on a team name and motto, we stress the importance of creating an identity based on qualities to which they should aspire. We ask students to submit only monikers and slogans that promote team spirit, respect, and great character. Previous years' names and slogans have included the following:

The Flying Pigs—"We do the impossible!"

The Asteroids—"Zooming through education!"

The Martians—"Learning is out of this world!"

Team Dynamite—"Get ready for a knowledge explosion!"

Setting the right tone for choosing an appropriate name and motto is important. We start by sending the memo shown in Figure 2.1.

Students compete to create the most appropriate team concept. As the company directors who have requested the advertising services, we select our five favorite designs. The finalists present their plans to the entire team, and the students select the concept that will define us as a team for the remainder of the year. However, we do not stop at selecting a name and a concept. We spend time during the next few weeks decorating and posting our motto in various locations within the team area and discussing how best to live up to its ideals. We do this in conjunction with team-building games that require students to work together to accomplish various tasks. These tasks may be

Sample Team Concept Memo

To: New Eighth-Grade Students
From: Management

The firm of MEW (Mayeaux, Edmonds, Wild) is searching for a group of experts to name their newly formed organization. We are happy that they have chosen our agency to represent them. They have promised a signing bonus (emergency fund credits) for the group that provides them with the best concept for their team organization.

The client, MEW, is looking for the following criteria in a team name and concept for their new classes:

1. **Originality**—No plagiarism of existing slogans, names, or ideas from any source. The concept must be totally original.
2. **Positive Image**—Only names and slogans that promote team spirit, respect, and great character will be considered.
3. **Neatness**—Logo should be pleasing to the eye and define the team's characteristics.
4. **Brevity**—Keep information short and loaded with "punch."

When compiling your portfolios for the client, be sure to include the following:

1. A **brief description** of the most important qualities in the new eighth-grade team. These should include qualities possessed by individual members that are assets of the entire team and qualities to which the team should aspire.
2. A **theme** that will bind the name, slogan, and logo. **The theme must have historical significance!**
3. A **team name** written (or typed) in a font that is complimentary to the name.
4. A **slogan** that corresponds with the team name and incorporates the goals and qualities of the team.
5. A **logo** drawn neatly and consistent with the team name, slogan, and qualities.

Selection Process:

1. The clients reserve the right to select the five best concepts.
2. The creative teams for the five chosen concepts will present their concepts to all stockholders.
3. The stockholders of the MEW organization will then vote by secret ballot for their favorite concept.
4. The MEW Corporation will announce the chosen team concept after voting has taken place.

Compensation/Wages:

As usual your compensation depends upon the quality of your work. There are no "hourly wages" involved in this project. You will receive one grade for the concept. Grades will reflect individual contributions to the group's activities. You will not be compensated for someone else's labor. These grades will be recorded in your ELT class. The members of groups with concepts chosen by the client as finalists will receive three emergency fund credits. The members of the group with the concept chosen to represent this year's team will receive six emergency credits to be used as needed.

Figure 2.1 Sample Team Concept Memo

intricate, such as going on a scavenger hunt around the school to collect clues to solve a mystery, or as simple as lining up in alphabetical order by middle name without speaking.

Every year we include academic connections based on the team name and concept in our core classes. When we were the Wizards, for example, we studied the history and literature of King Arthur and students named our team area Camelot. When we were known as the Flying Pigs, we found news articles about florescent green pigs being bred in other countries, information that we integrated into our language arts study of science fiction and our science unit dealing with genetics. Because our students are responsible for developing the team's identity and we integrate the themes into daily practices, they have a stronger connection to learning and to each other.

The "all for one" attitude that builds from the students' vested interest in the team results in a unique bond. We have seen students from opposite worlds not only become friends but also pull each other up academically and socially. Usually by November, we begin to hear our students speaking to each other as if they were family, not just classmates. We have witnessed everything from students giving each other ten-second pep talks to full-blown lectures on how to improve grades and behavior. The depth in which our students build their relationships with one another and become more of a family becomes apparent every year in the days leading to Christmas.

It has been a long-standing tradition for our students to read "The Gift of the Magi" and share ideas about the importance of giving during the holiday season. A few years ago we added to the tradition by asking students to write to one another about a gift they would share if they had no money to spend. It is truly amazing that these sincere, heartfelt letters every year focus on classroom-related topics, as opposed to superficial middle school interests. Martin, who was severely struggling in school, received this holiday gift from Shawn:

Dear Martin,

If I could give you anything in the world it would be my confidence because I think you are scared to learn around your friends. You probably think if you do your work they will make fun of you. But if you had my confidence you wouldn't worry about what other people say about you. When you're in class you learn, when you're outside of class you associate. In order to be something in life you have to go through school.

Sincerely,

Shawn

Some might argue that these relationship-building and team-naming activities take precious time away from the curriculum. This is true; we do not blast off from the beginning of the school year at rocket speed. But year after year we have found that the time and effort we spend getting acquainted with students saves us time in the long run. Because students learn to trust us and develop a better understanding of the purpose of learning, they are more willing to engage in deeper educational inquiry. By December we have always caught up to the curriculum timeline, and students are still interested in school events even after the newness of the school year has worn off. The initial relationship-building activities enable us to spend the remainder of the year focused on meaningful, integrated academic endeavors.

ChapterThree
Let's Get Acquainted

Building a relationship with the adolescent learner is a beginning point, but no teacher or team of teachers can manage the process alone. You have to have friends. Those friends include anyone who comes in contact with the child—from parents and grandparents to administrators, coaches, and ministers. Parents? Yes! The fallacy that families do not want to be involved in middle school students' lives prevails in our culture. We can prove it is not true.

Unfortunately we actually believed it ourselves at one time. We were extremely discouraged with family conferences that ended in conflict and produced limited solutions to problems. The turning point came after one particularly horrible conference in which a parent threatened to harm Monique and her children if she didn't change a student's grade. Monique pressed charges and filled out the required police paperwork, but not before she realized that she had to find a better method of communicating with students' families.

Having just completed the process to become certified by the National Board for Professional Teaching Standards, which emphasized the importance of reaching out to parents, Monique was moved to reflect on what had caused the meeting to end so badly. Although it would have been easier, and more satisfying, to simply conclude that the student's mother was crazy, Monique eventually realized that her own actions had contributed significantly to the conference's poor outcome. Monique had not had any contact with the parent prior to the conference. When the mother angrily complained about the child's grade, Monique became afraid, then defensive. She would not bend or work with the parent or the child to find a solution. She put the responsibility back on the family. Eventually, Monique realized that while she could not control the parent's reaction, she could change how she shared bad news with families and establish positive relationships throughout the year to build trust and reduce misunderstandings.

One of the major differences between our earlier approaches to working with families and our current practices is the way we try to involve them in team-building activities. Before jumping into detailed lesson plans and ideas for specific activities, we explore families' backgrounds and expectations. The first week of the new school year we send home surveys and ask for information to guide our work. See Figure 3.1 for an example.

This survey helps us plan appropriate instruction and provide necessary student supports. In addition, it immediately communicates to families that they are a valuable part of our team.

Families: Invite Them and Keep Them Coming Back

The relationships we build with families go beyond notes and phone calls. Our students' families are welcome additions to our team, and we want to see and hear from them regularly. The best way we've found to involve families and connect them to our team activities is to invite them to our classrooms. Our first personal meeting is a well-orchestrated effort known as our Let's Get Acquainted Night.

In 2002, our team was known as the Wizards. The invitation shown in Figure 3.2 went home with every Wizard on our team.

During the getting acquainted festivities, our students become experts who guide their parents through a typical school day—sort of a twist on the traditional open house in which teachers explain policies and procedures to family members as they rotate in and out of classrooms in small groups. Instead, our students present pertinent information, give examples of class activities, teach their families to solve math problems, introduce them to Internet resources that explain the state's standardized tests, and discuss classroom procedures. The students do such a marvelous job that we can cede the leadership role to them while we mingle and take photographs of the interactions.

Families truly want to be involved at school; they're just waiting for an invitation. Some parents and guardians who work odd shifts can't be present on a regular basis, but they make a good effort to show up for activities that directly involve their children. We remind them that the classroom doors are always open and that we appreciate any level of involvement.

When families can't come to the classroom, we try our best to bring the classroom to them. We send email messages that contain links to students' work samples, video clips, and PowerPoint presentations. For those parents who do

Family Survey

We look forward to working with your child this school year. We will spend the first weeks doing activities to help us get to know your child's personal and academic interests. Please answer the following questions and return this sheet to school tomorrow. Thank you for assisting us in working with your child. If you ever need to contact us, please do. You may reach us by calling the school or via our website at www.edline.net. (You must obtain a password from the office to access Edline.)

We anticipate a terrific year working with you and your child.

Sincerely,

Kathryn Edmonds, Monique Wild, & Amanda Mayeaux

Child's Name: _____

Your Name: _____

How often does your child read at home?
___ Never ___ Only when necessary ___ Once a month ___ Once a week ___ More than once a week

What do you notice about your child's reading habits?

What do you notice about your child's language skills (writing and speaking)?

What are your child's favorite hobbies?

What should we know about your child?

Do you and your child discuss historical issues?

Does your child keep track of current events?

Does your child try to solve real-world math problems (estimate grocery bills, figure miles per gallon, etc.)?

In which type of extracurricular activities does your child participate?

Has your child ever used a public library? Why?

Does your household have access to the Internet and email?

If you would like to receive our weekly updates via email, please provide your email address here:

_____

Figure 3.1 Sample Family Survey

Let's Get Acquainted Night

The Wizards cordially invite you to an enchanted evening in Camelot where your very own Wizard will introduce you to the magic that sparkles daily in our classrooms.

On September 9, 2002, at 5:30 p.m., we would like to invite you and your child to attend a special meeting for our team. This meeting will last until 7:30 p.m.

During this meeting, our team of Wizards (your children) will assist us in answering some of the following questions:

· How can I help my child do well on the LEAP?
· What resources are there to help with the LEAP?
· What is Writer's Workshop?
· What is Reader's Workshop?
· What kind of problem-solving is my child doing?
· What types of things is my child doing in science?
· What does the curriculum require my child to master?
· Why did I buy that really BIG binder?

Figure 3.2 Invitation to Let's Get Acquainted Night

not have access to email and technology, we make alternative arrangements. For example, if parents couldn't view the Valentine's Day presentations on their home computers, we saved the work on a CD-ROM so they could view them on computers at the local library. In addition, during our regularly scheduled student-led conferences, which we call Portfolio Show-Off Day, we had computers available for parents to view their children's work. After sharing the PowerPoint Valentine's Day messages with snippets of student-written poetry, we received many positive responses from parents.

"The poems touched my heart deeply," Austin's mother wrote back. "They're certainly a forever keepsake! Thanks for all you do to tap into the whole child and to help them reach their fullest potential!"

If we want our students to reach their fullest potential, we must involve their families in the learning process. We spend a great deal of time teaching our students how to discuss education issues with their families so everyone will understand the importance of lifelong learning. Portfolio Show-Off Day is a great opportunity for our students to practice these communication skills.

During one memorable Portfolio Show-Off Day, the hallway was bustling with parents and students chattering about their work. We set up desks along both sides of the length of the hallway so parents and students could chat with each other easily. Allison's dad was standing beside her mom, laughing at a short story their daughter had written. Jeremy's brother had pulled up an extra chair to listen to Jeremy's tape recording of the class's choral reading of "The Highwayman." At the end of the hall two grandparents had joined several others in viewing the silent films the children had created. Other visitors wandered around looking at all the student work that represented a year in the life of our learners.

At one point in the evening, Amanda walked out of her classroom to check on some activities and was surprised to see Ricardo's mother weeping in the hallway. Ricardo was gently rubbing his mother's hand and soothing her with quiet assurances.

Amanda rushed over to the parent and asked, "Are you okay?"

Ricardo's mother looked up and said, "I ain't never been here before, but nobody told me my boy was so smart. I should have come sooner."

Building on the Love

Parents love their children, but not all of them have fond memories of school. Some of them stay away from school because they fear that their children will have similarly miserable experiences and they don't want to relive the pain. After struggling to connect with parents over the years and having some yell at us over the telephone or refuse to sign and return paperwork, we knew we had to get to know them better before they would trust us enough to help their children.

During our first year teaming together, we decided to make family relationships a priority. When we dug deeper through conversations, surveys, and email correspondence into the issues that kept parents from visiting school, we found stories of illiterate parents who were embarrassed about being unable to sign their names or those who simply thought they had nothing to contribute. As teachers our job is to change that perspective. No parent should have to wait until the end of middle school to discover a child's talents, as Ricardo's mother did. If we're doing our job well, information and insights about students should flow back and forth between school and home in a continuous loop of learning and sharing.

Young adolescents can be critical conduits in this communication cycle. It's true that middle school students routinely toss report cards, permission slips, and other important paperwork for parents into their backpacks, along with empty potato chip bags, iPods, and dirty gym shorts. Many of the messages intended for home inspection never reach their destinations. This can be a source of irritation for both parents and teachers as each awaits a response that the other didn't know was needed. If the backpack express is the only method teams use to share news about students' progress and problems, the results will be inconsistent and unsatisfactory.

At the same time, we firmly believe that young adolescents can be taught to be responsible and accountable. One of the key ways we build their skills and enlist their support in strengthening home/school connections is through student-led conferences, which involve students and their parents discussing work samples and academic progress. Although teachers are intimately involved in this process, the students lead the discussions. We have found that if we truly want our students to feel in control and become responsible for the conference, it is best if we are available to clarify points without actually sitting in on the entire conference.

According to Donald Hackmann (1997) student-led conferences enable students to take an active role in discussing academic progress, which encourages them to be more accountable about their progress to their parents and teachers. Hackmann identifies three phases of student-led conferences, which we always include in our practices: preparation, conferencing, and evaluation.

I would rate my child's sense of responsibility what on a scale of 1-10 why?

Plan for my discussion with my parents/guardians

1. Three things I want to discuss with my parents are ...

2. What I need to explain to my parents about my goals includes ...

3. The thing that I'm most proud of is ...

4. I need to work on ...

5. I want to tell my parents that I need help with ...

6. I want to tell my parents thank you for ...

Figure 3.3 Plan for Student-Led Conference with Parents/Guardians

Preparation

Preparation for student-led conferences on our team includes collecting artifacts, reviewing and self-evaluating the artifacts, planning discussion points, and practicing conference procedures. Beginning with the first day of school our students keep a portfolio that contains *every* graded assignment, quarterly goals they set for themselves, interest and learning style surveys, photographs, newspaper articles, self-evaluations and improvement plans, and computer-generated grade report summaries. The portfolios not only become great tools for tracking students' successes (and sometimes failures); the collections also provide insights about our classroom activities.

Typically we set aside three days or nights throughout the school year for Portfolio Show-Off and student-led conferences. Parents sign up for time slots during which they come to view their child's portfolio and have a conference with their child. Although we are available to answer general questions, we do not use this time for private conferences to discuss students' behavior or grades. These events are strictly for the students to share their efforts and explain why they may be behind. Because we stay well into the evening on these days, working parents also have the opportunity to share this experience with their children.

Conferencing

Carol Smith (n.d.) emphasizes that student-led conferences should go well beyond a display of the year's activities and lessons. The conferences should focus primarily on students' reflection and growth. To guide students through this process, we help them develop a plan to lead their discussions with their families and ensure that the conferences are productive, meaningful, and enlightening. The format for the plan changes periodically but always follows the basic pattern shown in Figure 3.3. The plan is accompanied by a cover letter reminding families about the purpose of the conference (see Figure 3.4).

We never encounter low attendance when we invite families to school for student-led conferences. On average about 75 percent of our students' families make themselves available to attend Portfolio Show-Off Day compared to the 25 percent we saw when we just requested a conference when a student had problems. The high turnout for student-led conferences, a trend supported by research (Hackmann 1997), doesn't happen automatically. We send notes and email messages and make phone calls until we are certain that every parent has received information about the events. We emphasize the importance of the process, and students' excitement about sharing their progress bubbles over at home as well. If families cannot attend the events, we send their children's portfolios home.

Dear Parents and Guardians:

Welcome to our Portfolio Show-Off Day! We are so glad that you are able to be here with your child today. We are dedicated to keeping you informed about your child's progress. We hope that this conference with your child proves enlightening.

While you are here viewing your child's portfolio, please take time to look at the quality of your child's work. Praise your child for his or her accomplishments and make plans for improvements.

Items that you should ask your child about include:

1. Portfolios
2. Reading journals
3. Planners
4. Reading homework charts
5. The book that he/she is currently reading
6. Self-evaluations for the current grading period
7. Anything else you've been dying to find out

Also, we'd like to remind you that we update our website every week with class assignments. You may visit us at www.edline.net.

Sincerely,

The Flying Pigs

Figure 3.4 Sample Student-Led Conference Cover Letter

Evaluation

Following each portfolio event, we request feedback from parents and students. Figure 3.5 provides a sample feedback form.

From the feedback forms we learned that parents were not getting our communications, so we began calling home when notes were not returned, sending email messages to families who had Internet access, and sending second notices through the postal service.

The feedback forms also relay information about problems, illnesses, and tragedies that our students experience, as well as the reasons why some hate school. The history and insights help us understand why students may misbehave or struggle.

We also stopped assigning take-home projects after many families told us how much they loathed them. Some parents resented how these projects encroached on their hectic schedules and limited family time. Others said they lacked the money to buy necessary materials or the knowledge to help their children complete the projects. When it became clear that class projects were causing major disruptions, we changed our approach. We now live by the idea that if something is worth doing, we will provide time to complete it in class. We still assign homework, but major projects happen in our classrooms.

Because families can't visit school every day, we keep them up-to-date through our team website. We provide links to other Internet resources that reinforce skills and information taught in the classroom. Currently, our school district uses the Web service Edline, which provides password-protected access to students' grades, class assignments, and daily handouts. There are many other similar services, such as schoolnotes. com and teacherweb.com, which are easy to use and economical.

Child's Name: _____

Parents,

Please respond to the following questions so that we might be able to plan for future contacts.

1. How was the student/parent conference beneficial to you and your child?

2. What was the most pertinent information that you gained?

3. What do you still want to know?

4. What were your expectations of the event prior to conferencing with your child?

5. What do you feel your child's teachers need to know?

Figure 3.5 Student-Led Conference Feedback Form

Building a Web of Support

Whether we communicate with our students' families in person, via the telephone, or in writing, we spread the message that their children are special to us. Whenever we contact parents or guardians, we follow the same format:

1. Say something positive (you may have to dig deep).
2. State what happened and how the student's behavior is keeping him (and, potentially, his peers) from learning.
3. Say something positive (you may have to dig deeper).

For example, instead of saying, "Johnny talks all the time during class. He never takes notes, and if he doesn't get it under control he'll fail the unit," we might take a different approach. "Good afternoon, Mrs. Doe. I'm just calling to let you know how Johnny has been doing in class. He is one of our most outgoing students, really friendly to everyone in the class. Recently he has been forgetting to take his notes and practice the sample problems. I know how much you and your husband want Johnny to succeed, so I'm sure you'll be encouraging him at home to work to his full potential in the classroom, and he can still be just as sociable at recess."

Another approach we use is to make the introductory and closing remarks and let the student tell her mom or dad what she's been up to. This idea occurred to us after we had many phone conversations with parents who didn't believe our account of their children's misbehaviors. We thought (correctly, as it turned out) that if the students heard the disappointment or anger in their parents' voices, they might be more motivated to immediately correct their behavior. One such conversation went as follows:

"Hello, Mr. Davis, this is Kathryn Edmonds, Lance's teacher, calling from Dutchtown Middle School. Today in math class we are learning several probability concepts, which are not only going to be on Lance's nine-weeks exam but also on the statewide assessment in three weeks. This is usually a tough unit for students, and I know how well you expect Lance to perform. Lance is here with me now, and I'm going to let him talk to you and share how he's been using his time in math class this morning."

"Dad, this is Lance. I haven't been doing my work this morning, and now my teacher is upset. (PAUSE) No, sir, I didn't write any of the notes. (PAUSE) Nope, I didn't do the activity either. (PAUSE) Well, uh, I was sleeping at first; then when she woke me up, I didn't know what we were doing, so I started tearin' up paper and throwin' it on the floor. (LONG PAUSE) He wants to talk to you again, Mrs. Edmonds."

"Hey, Mr. Davis, it's Kathryn again."

"Mrs. Edmonds, I am so sorry you had to call me to get Lance to finally focus in class. I would like a copy of the notes and the activity, and Lance will complete everything tonight, twice if it's not perfect the first time!"

"Yes, sir, I hate that I had to call you, too, but I know you only want the best for your son."

"Yes, ma'am, thank you, and please know this will not happen again. But if he starts to slip, please don't hesitate to call me anytime."

"Thank you, Mr. Davis. Have a good rest of the day."

Lance took notes and completed all of his activities for a solid eight weeks (a major achievement for a special education student with an individualized education plan [IEP] that included a behavior plan).

Our multifaceted team effort to build bonds between school and home has made an astounding difference in our interactions with students' families. Establishing and maintaining strong, positive relationships with parents and guardians is a conscious part of our work, never an afterthought. They are vital partners in education, and we no longer take them for granted.

The degree to which our relationships have changed became clear in the summer of 2006, as we were preparing our presentation for the Disney American Teacher Awards. During our deliberations, we realized that we needed a video clip of Markeith. We called his home to request the opportunity to film him during the next week. Markeith's mom responded, "You need Markeith? Yes, Mrs. Mayeaux, we will take him to you right now."

Ten minutes later, Markeith's brother dropped him off at Monique's house, and we completed the videotaping. Only when Markeith was about to leave did we learn the entire story. Markeith had been on his way to a doctor's appointment when we called. His mother quickly rescheduled

---

Contact Cards

Whether you need to contact families because of an emergency or because their children are being disruptive, you will want to have quick access to phone numbers and email addresses. Compile this information on half sheets of card stock paper, bound with a single ring, and hang the collection at a designated place in each classroom. Make sure substitute teachers know how to find the cards. To keep this information confidential and out of students' reach, we hang the cards facing backward above our filing cabinet.

Sample Contact Card

Student's Name: _____

Lives With: _____

Home Phone Number: _____

Work/Cell Number: _____

Email Address: _____

Alternate Contact 1: _____

Alternate Contact 2: _____

the appointment and rerouted him to Monique's house because "his teachers needed him."

That kind of parental support is invaluable to a teaching team. It is worth the time and effort to cultivate such relationships because they enrich us personally and professionally. Our relationships with students' families are based on mutual concern for the most important people in the parents' lives—their children. We have found that our students' families go out of their way to support our decisions because they know how much we care for their children.

Relationships with Administrators: Friends in High Places

Although we'd love to claim responsibility for every positive aspect of our teaching relationships, the truth is that we wouldn't be as successful without our school administrators' support. They create so many opportunities to build rapport with students and their families. Because the principal, Doug Walker, is willing to stay after school to lock up, we can extend student-led conferences into the evening hours. Because he sets an open-door policy, families feel welcome to visit our classrooms whenever they choose, as long as they notify the office that they are in the building. Because Susan Jordan, our assistant principal, makes time to observe the baby rats born to the pets in our science class, our students believe that administrators care about what they are learning.

In return for this support and assistance, the principal simply requests that we run our ideas for "extra activities" by him before we send notices to students' families. After all, he is the person responsible for everyone on campus. And because of legal issues, he must view our plans through a different lens than we do. More than once, he has told us in jest, "Some of the most frightening words from you three are, 'We have a great idea!'"

The principal has disallowed some of our grand schemes. We'd be lying if we said we weren't disappointed. It can be very frustrating to hear "no" when you are trying to arrange a project or event that you consider crucial to students' learning. But before you go on a rampage or view the decision as a personal attack, remember that the administrator knows more about the intricate workings of the school community than you do. Tunnel vision is easy to develop when you are confined to the classroom every day.

If you believe your idea is worth fighting for (as we often do), try approaching the principal, dean, counselor, or department chair again. Respectfully request another meeting and thoroughly explain why your plans are necessary and will benefit your students. Listen to the supervisor's reasons for denying your request and then suggest a compromise that maintains the integrity of your idea and addresses his or her concerns. Sometimes this approach will result in a revised idea going forward; sometimes the plan still won't work. However things turn out, the administrators will appreciate that you respected their authority and did not proceed without following the proper protocols.

Administrators really need to be informed about successful endeavors as well as problems. Because they deal with the public, they need accurate information to convey. We routinely invite administrators to special team events, presentations, and conferences. We extend an open invitation to visit our classrooms at any time and become involved in the lessons we are teaching. Often the principal and assistant principal will walk through our classrooms to check on certain students, and they will praise these students' work when they see them elsewhere on campus.

If teaming demonstrates nothing else, it definitely supports the belief that more can be accomplished as a group than individually. Effective teams realize that time spent building positive, satisfying relationships with students, parents, and administrators pays off in the long run by creating a culture that supports teaching and learning. Such relationships free teachers to focus on the real work of education—providing instructional experiences that help students succeed.

ChapterFour
Creating a Culture of Achievement

As the World War II veteran recounted his role in the invasion of Normandy, tears streamed from thirteen-year-old Greg's eyes.

"Thank you," Greg said as he jotted notes.

"Son," the veteran replied, "I tell the story every day, and I cry every time."

Our students were at The National World War II Museum in New Orleans to gather information for our team's study of life during the 1940s. As they toured the museum, the students examined the displays and interacted with the veterans who work there. They carried clipboards and took notes to share with one another when they returned to school.

Most impressive throughout the day was our students' level of involvement. They stopped to appreciate every exhibit and took time to imagine the events depicted there. Several people commented on the students' attentiveness and good behavior. One visitor, who had witnessed the interaction between Greg and the Normandy veteran, turned to Monique and said, "I've been watching your students. They have such intelligent questions. It is obvious they already know a lot about World War II. They are so involved and well behaved. They must be your school's most advanced class."

Brian and Ashton, two of the students who heard the woman's praise, smiled and giggled at the comment. A smile spread across Greg's face. The students exchanged a quick glance with Monique. She winked at the students and then thanked the woman for noticing their efforts.

"Yes," Monique said. "They are extremely intelligent and very well behaved when they choose to be."

Contrary to the woman's assumptions, our students would not have been considered advanced by any traditional measure. All forty-four were members of our school's Challenge program, which was designed to put struggling students on a fast track to high school. Each student had been retained twice during elementary school and was at risk of dropping out before becoming part of our teaching team in the seventh grade. They were overage and unmotivated. A year later, at the time of the museum visit, they had made up the equivalent of two grade levels and had begun looking at failure through the rearview window.

Their path to progress was rocky and uneven. Our performance as their teachers provided plenty of pitfalls too. But the journey to reach that point proved to be the most rewarding school year of our careers, and the lessons from those experiences have enriched our work, offering valuable insights about how effective teaching teams can change young adolescents' futures.

Every teacher struggles to reach all of his or her students. One of the great myths of education is that learning is linear, with each new idea linked to the previous one like colorful and connected towers of Lego blocks. According to this theory, a teacher needs only to fit this piece to that piece to construct the curriculum, and the lessons will seep into students' brains steadily and surely. Reality is much messier than that.

For example, though we pride ourselves on reaching out to students who build walls around themselves and balk in the face of anything remotely educational, some have slipped through our grasp. Recall from Chapter 1 our struggle with a student who was going to be expelled for discipline issues and for repeatedly leaving campus during the school day. Looking back, we realize that we became emotional with each other because we had invested so much time and energy trying to turn this student around. We had spent months counseling, cajoling, encouraging, befriending, conferencing, teaching, and begging him to make wise decisions. However, in the end, he rejected our help, including the final appeal we made to the expulsion committee on his behalf. Eventually, the school dismissed him.

We could have become discouraged by our failure to save this student from his self-destructive impulses. Instead, we chose to focus on what he had accomplished during our time together, reflect on some missed opportunities, and use this knowledge to improve our practices. The same student, prior to his expulsion, had helped his peers with math problems, stayed after school to sweep our classrooms, and brought his brother to meet his teachers. Academically, he had stints of success. For a whole week, he turned in every homework assignment. He wrote full-page entries in his journals. He floated around the class during math to assist other students. Success, for some, must be measured in small steps forward.

However, he was unable to maintain these efforts. We discovered that education was not valued in his family. Most of his siblings had actually raised their esteem within the family by dropping out of school to go to work. Because our student was too young to drop out legally, he figured out another way to disengage from school. Ultimately, we did not have the power to keep him in.

Learning to Value Education

Schools today are full of students who are struggling for one reason or another. And they can't all be lumped together into one stereotypical pool of poverty and ethnicity. Before you begin to conjure thoughts that students at risk of failure only inhabit the hallways of urban schools, consider this frightening image. In *On Common Ground* (DuFour, Eaker, and DuFour, eds. 2005), Roland Barth and his colleagues define at-risk students as those who are unlikely to continue learning once they leave school. Barth's explanation suggests that both average achievers and gifted students from "Beaver Cleaver" homes may be in danger of disconnecting if they don't receive the right stimulation and support in school.

Several years ago, when we began examining national and school data as a starting point for our investigation of the common causes of student failure, we were stunned by what we found. For example, we discovered that in 1997–1998, only 30.5 percent of students seventeen years old and older with learning disabilities held a standard high school diploma (U.S. Department of Education 2000). At Dutchtown Middle School, we were on track to continue that awful trend. At the time, just 11 percent of our school's special needs students scored at the proficient level on the state assessments, which meant they were in danger of repeating a grade. In addition, many of our students in the Challenge program—not all of them with identified learning disabilities—had already repeated grade levels while in elementary school. Research suggested that this factor alone made them twenty times more likely to drop out of school than students who are on pace when they enter the middle grades (Rumberger 1995). Other studies have found that one grade retention increases a student's risk of dropping out by 40 to 50 percent, while being retained two grade levels increases the risk by 90 percent (Roderick 1995). Such a frightening statistic underscores our critically important roles as middle-level educators.

As a team, we have tried a range of class configurations to combat failure, including separating a large group of underachievers for accelerated instruction, as we did with the Challenge group during the 2005–2006 school year. We also have tried blending special needs students into our regular classes instead of placing them in self-contained sessions, as well as teaching the same group of students for two years to provide more consistent instruction and build on secure, established relationships. Every year we analyze the strengths and weaknesses of the students whom we inherit and try to find a team arrangement that will be most beneficial.

But appropriate groupings are only one part of the solution for struggling students. An equally crucial component is showing them how to learn. Many students enter middle school behind in one category or another. They may have limited language skills, social and emotional gaps, inadequate family support, or weak foundations in one subject or many. Addressing those deficiencies takes teamwork and a determined approach to meet students where they are and move them ahead, whether by inches or leaps.

Students closely watch their teachers—even when the adolescents seem preoccupied with a dozen nonacademic distractions—so it's important for us to model effective learning habits. One day, for example, Amanda loudly and purposefully stacked three novels, four academic books, six academic journals, seven newspapers, three trade magazines, and two articles downloaded from the Internet on top of the overhead projector in the front of her classroom. The students were so perplexed that they just sat and stared. They had been expecting to begin their math lesson as soon as they entered the room.

Amanda stood by the stack and said, "This represents the information I have read this week. I am a learner and, as such, I am in constant need of new knowledge. My appetite is never satisfied. Let me share a few things I have found out this week from my adventures in text."

Amanda continued for the next five minutes sharing what she had learned about how a student's brain processes new information, the life of the ancient Romans, and the unbelievable carnage at the Battle of Gettysburg.

"So, you read all of that?" asked Charles.

"No, I did not read every word in every one of these books, but as a learner I used specific skills to find what interested me," Amanda responded. "I browsed the tables of contents in the books or I used the index to find what might interest me."

Amanda then shared how she might read an entire article from one magazine and highlight important information, while in another magazine she might just skim the material for key ideas.

"Do you ever sleep?" April asked, laughing.

"Well, I know if I have a book with me, I am never alone, so I read everywhere and whenever I have time," Amanda said. "For example, yesterday when y'all went to lunch, I had twenty minutes to read through this article on deer populations, which we will use soon in our class. Reading is something I find time to do."

In the back corner of the room, Charles raised his hand to ask, "But you are a math teacher; what does this have to do with math?"

Amanda replied, "Being a math teacher is second to my being a learner. If I am not learning, how can I expect you to do so? I don't have the money or the time to fly off to Rome, but I can read about it. Reading is my transport vehicle, my time machine, so to speak. I can go anywhere at any time. I also love to talk about what I am learning, which is another habit of voracious learners. So, I will share what I am reading throughout the year, and I in turn expect you to share with me."

The students sat and pondered these ideas very thoughtfully. Although it would take time for many of them to believe in the value of reading in multiple disciplines, the seeds were planted that day.

Such examples and explanations are crucial for middle grades students, especially for those who do not live in homes where reading for pleasure and academic discussions are part of the family's routines. Amanda's reading demonstration is one of the many short activities we use at the beginning of the school year to set the standard for meaningful learning. Our instructional plans would be pointless if we did not also provide daily reminders and examples of how scholars reflect, debate, synthesize, evaluate, and deepen their understanding as they develop intrinsic motivation to explore the world.

One of our team's formative goals is establishing an insatiable hunger for learning. We believe the best way to stimulate students' academic appetites is by providing a rich intellectual diet. But first, we have to persuade them to try things they may have found distasteful in the past.

For many students, poor reading skills interfere with academic success in all subject areas. When we taught the Challenge program, 75 percent of our students started the year with scores below the fiftieth percentile level on a national, norm-referenced test of reading skills. Clarissa was typical of many students who had developed defiant attitudes to mask their frustrations. When she entered Monique's language arts class in August, she placed one hand on her hip, flashed her fingers in front of her face in a Hollywood-quality Z-snap, and said, "My sister said you make people like to read. Well, I hate to read, and I ain't gonna read no book!"

Monique simply smiled and replied, "You will read before the year is over, I promise. There are tons of excellent books out there, and I'm sure the right one is waiting for you somewhere. I'll help you find it."

Clarissa backed down just a little. "I know you're gonna make me read, but I ain't gonna like it!" she said.

By January of the same school year, Clarissa had recorded a message for our team literacy campaign in which she excitedly stated, "Reading is fun if you know how, so get a book, snuggle up, and read!" Here was the queen of the antireading crowd working to persuade others that it was a worthwhile activity!

Literate—and Lovin' it!

Clarissa's transformation was not instantaneous, miraculous, or isolated. It resulted from a calculated team effort to place reading center stage in all subject areas. From the first day of school, we design activities to infuse literacy throughout the curriculum.

Sometimes the methods prompt students to question our motives and doubt our sanity. Two weeks into one school year, Ashley quietly confided in Amanda, "I don't want to be mean, but I think Mrs. Wild is very A.D.D. Maybe she needs medicine."

"What do you mean?" Amanda asked, pretending not to know why the student thought Monique had attention deficit disorder.

"Well, she keeps jumping from thing to thing in class," Ashley explained. "She keeps starting this movie and three minutes into it, she turns it off and says, 'Let's do something else.' I don't know if she is right, Mrs. Mayeaux. You might need to check on her."

Kathryn, who had overheard the exchange, stifled a giggle. Both she and Amanda knew what Monique was up to. In the middle of a lesson, Monique would say, "I don't feel like doing this any more. Let's watch a movie!" Of course, the students were willing to stop the lesson to watch a movie, so Monique put a *Star Wars* DVD into the player and let the credits roll. As soon as the first character appeared in the movie, Monique said, "Aw, this isn't making any sense. Let's go back to work." Without any explanation, she then continued the class as if there hadn't been any interruption.

Monique followed this pattern for four days. She would stop the lesson midstream to resume the movie, only to turn it off after complaining about being bored or not understanding the plot. When Kathryn was in the classroom, she would sympathize with the students and beg to watch more of the movie right along with them. When the students moved to Amanda's class, she patiently listened to their complaints and controlled her desire to laugh.

Monique went about the school day as though nothing was amiss, but on the sly she was recording the comments students made:

"If you would let it play, you'd understand it."

"You can't watch two minutes at a time; you'll never get it."

"You have to give it a chance. Don't just give up on the story."

"The first five minutes is just the setting and the characters. They haven't even gotten to the plot!"

"You'll never get through it like this."

"Have you ever watched a movie? This is *not* how you do it!"

Finally, on the fifth day, Monique decided that watching a new movie was in order. She popped *Indiana Jones and the Temple of Doom* into the machine and said, "I know what the problem is. *Star Wars* is a bad movie. Let's try *Indiana Jones*."

Of course, *Indiana Jones* met the same fate as *Star Wars*, and a new cycle of interrupted and disconnected activities began. By this point our students were beside themselves with frustration. "Why are you doing this?" they asked. "You are picking good movies; you're just not watching enough of them. The problem is not the movie; it's the way you're watching it."

Jean Paul timidly ventured an idea: "I know. You're trying to make a point about something, aren't you?" he asked.

"About what?" Monique answered with another question.

"I don't know," Jean Paul replied. "But something about language or reading since this is language arts."

"Oh!" exclaimed Tate, picking up the conversation thread. "You're showing us what *not* to do."

"What not to do when?" Monique asked, purposely obtuse.

"When we read?" asked Tate.

"Yes," Monique said, "and you have supplied me with all the lessons I wanted you to learn about reading."

Kathryn began to read from the list of student comments that Monique had compiled, and the students groaned. They had been fooled into creating the list of arguments that we would use the rest of the year to encourage them to read. Here are some of the lessons the students discovered:

- Give books a chance and you might just find a story you like.
- Spend time reading. It is impossible to get involved in a story if you only spend a couple of minutes with it.

- Read at least a third of the book before you give up. The beginning of the book builds the plot by introducing characters, establishing the setting, and so on. The early part of the story or book might not be as exciting as the middle, but it helps you understand the meaning.
- Don't skip from book to book. Spend time finding a story that interests you so that you won't abandon every book you pick up.
- Books are like movies; they're stories. If you like movies, you may just enjoy reading a book.

Our effort to captivate young readers does not end with this little bit of fun. If we want our students to love reading, we have to link literacy to every subject. We also use reading to reinforce skills, such as cooperation, that help our team function effectively.

Seedfolks, by Paul Fleischman (1999), is a wonderful, short book that we have used to teach students how different people with different ideas can come together to make a community. We do not relegate the book to Monique's language arts classes. Because we want to demonstrate the strong connections in a community, we each read a few chapters a day to whichever group we have after lunch. The book's lessons would not resonate if we simply read a passage and then walked away, so we extend the classroom conversation through dialogue journals. In addition, we may make simple academic connections such as asking students to plant bean seeds in our small team garden during science class. We talk about how we jointly care for the plants, which leads to discussions about how we could grow if we all worked together. These conversations, in turn, lead to others that examine the qualities of supportive communities. Through such exchanges, our students realize that what they read and learn applies to their lives.

As Joey reflected in his journal, "I think the quote hanging in Mrs. Wild's room that says, 'Never doubt that a small group of thoughtful, committed citizens can change the world . . . ' relates to the book *Seedfolks* that we read in Mrs. Mayeaux's class. In *Seedfolks*, they changed their town and how people treated each other. I think it relates to our class because we do stuff to help each other and the community."

That year, when we had finished reading *Seedfolks* aloud, our students missed the daily habit. So Amanda began reading *Tangerine*, by Edward Bloor (1997), in her math classes. Students started rushing in the door each day to get their ten-minute literary fix.

As the story progresses, the book takes a sad turn when one of the characters dies. During class, Amanda read the following passage: "Erik stopped just inside the garage and said, 'Mike Costello is dead, Mom. He got killed at practice today.'" Then she closed the book.

"What?" students yelled, wanting more.

"That's it," Amanda said. "That is all I am reading to you. If you want to know what happened, you will have to get the book and read it."

The screaming match began.

"Where can we get one?" students cried out in unison.

"It just so happens I have nine copies right here," Amanda said, "and I will draw names for anyone interested in finishing the book over the weekend."

When twenty students threw their hands into the air, Amanda wrote their names on slips of paper. After the drawing, Joey was not among those who had received a classroom copy.

"They have to be done by Monday, right?" he asked. "Well, I will just go buy my own."

Joey and many others did buy their own copies of *Tangerine*, including several students who told us that they had made their first visit to a bookstore during the weekend. Their enthusiasm reminded us of the pivotal moments during our own adolescence when reading became a passion—and of the adults who either spurred our interest or snuffed it out.

Amanda recalled the librarian who refused to let her borrow a copy of *Gone with the Wind*. Kathryn told us how she had to wait until the twelfth grade to find a teacher who made her excited about literature, and Monique revealed that she had struggled to comprehend anything she read before the fourth grade. Though she could read the words, her fluency often interfered with understanding. The lack of positive experiences and her perception that reading was out of her grasp caused Monique to avoid books whenever possible.

Monique's view of reading changed when her grandmother took her to the library one summer and helped Monique select a "thick book," which she then read cover to cover. Her grandmother checked with Monique daily to see what she thought about *Johnny Appleseed*, the book she'd chosen. During their conversations, Monique's grandmother revealed that she, too, had read *Johnny Appleseed* as a child and told of her favorite events in the plot. The conversations carried Monique through the book, at first because she did not want to disappoint her grandmother and eventually because she wanted to find out what happened next in the story. The powerful combination of good literature, authentic interactions with another reader, and pride in finishing an entire book helped Monique become a passionate reader.

Reflecting on this life event caused Monique to decide that as a teacher she wanted to show her students how to love reading just as her grandmother had taught her. Now, because we work as a team, our students experience three adults supporting them in the way Monique's grandmother supported her and illustrated the joys of reading for her. This occurs for all of the reading they complete in class, both independent reading for enjoyment and assigned reading for class.

Reading Becomes a Habit

The reading we typically assign in our classes consists of literature that encourages deep thinking. We read short stories such as "The Lady or the Tiger" by Frank Stockton (1884), which drives our students crazy because of its inconclusive ending. Months later they continue to debate the story during class, at lunch, and during recess. We read novels such as *The Outsiders* by S. E. Hinton (1967), which pull our students into the action before they even realize they're reading. In addition to assigning poignant literature, we consciously seek to develop students' reading habits by letting them make informed choices about what they will read.

Early in our collaboration, we used Nancie Atwell's book *In the Middle* as an idea generator for our team practices. As Atwell explains, students become more enthusiastic about reading when they get to choose what they read and have access to a wide selection of text.

We took this message to heart and began surrounding our students with great literature of all genres. Our team now has a library of more than one thousand titles, which are arranged alphabetically by the author's last name and housed in Monique's classroom. When students need resources or a book to read, they first check the team library and then visit the school library if necessary. However, our students do not just randomly choose the books they'll read from our shelf. Without guidance, they would spend most of their time shuffling from shelf to shelf randomly choosing books to read. Without proper background knowledge about the types of books available to them, our students cannot make informed decisions as they select books to read.

To help students match books to their interests and make a plan for their potential reading, we use a variety of techniques. First, our students maintain a list of favorite authors, genres, and books. Once they identify the books they enjoy and the factors contributing to their enjoyment, they are more likely to seek books that they are predisposed to like. In addition, our students maintain a list of books they want to read so that they always have specific books they can look for on the crowded shelves without resorting to random choices that hold no significance for them.

Using book talks, we recommend books we've enjoyed to students by listing the criteria for quality. Our students listen to the talks and make recommendations for books they've read that are similar. Sometimes our students have read the books we're introducing, and they reveal their experiences with the books as well. Eventually, our students will take over the book talks and the job of persuading their classmates to read the books they've enjoyed.

In addition to book talks, we often give our students a chance to sample various books from the class library. We place one book on each student's desk. We then provide two minutes for students to peruse the books and make notations. At the end of two minutes our students either add the book to their must-read list, or pass it on to the next student in the row. The books continue around the classroom in a round-robin fashion until students have been exposed to ten to fifteen books during the session. We have found that once students discover the types of books that interest them and begin relating those books to other life and school experiences, they are hooked.

Reading eventually becomes a habit for our students, which is the first step to becoming avid readers. But good habits must be cultivated through structure, guidance, and practice. We hold our students accountable for reading twenty minutes each day during class and twenty minutes at home each night. We track their progress by recording page numbers as our students silently read in class. Each night our students record the number of the last page they've read, and we check their charts the following day during our twenty minutes of independent reading.

In addition to monitoring students' reading progress, we take the time to discuss the books with them during brief asides in class. We also often ask them to use journal entries to relate independent reading to assigned reading by asking questions such as, "What have you read independently that reminds you of the short story 'Flowers for Algernon'? Explain how the two pieces of literature are related."

Ultimately, we want our students to explore books of their own choosing to experience what Teri Lesesne calls the "unconscious delight" of reading that occurs when we become absorbed in books. In *Making the Match* (2003), Lesene describes the stages students pass through on their way to becoming lifelong readers. These steps include reading autobiographically to search for characters like themselves, reading for philosophical speculation, and reading for aesthetic and vicarious experiences.

Time is a crucial stimulus for enthusiastic readers. "Frequent practice in reading is one of the main contributors to developing fluency," David A. Sousa reminds us in *How the Brain Learns to Read*. "Children who lack fluency read slowly and laboriously, often making it difficult for them to remember what has been read and to relate the ideas expressed in the text to their own experiences" (2005a, 82).

The impact of focusing on reading across the team amazes us year after year. Our toughest group of students produced the most surprising results. Of the forty-four students in the Challenge program, only six had read a novel independently before joining our team. The others had listened to books on tape in class but had not actually read for themselves. By the end of the school year, they were reading a book every two weeks, on average. Some students read one book a week, a few read a book every three weeks, but every student significantly improved.

This is not to say that we consider quantity the only evidence of success, but the more students read, the more fluent they become. Our students also developed new perspectives about reading's benefits.

Joshua visited us on his first day of high school to reveal his discovery to Monique. "You know, Mrs. Wild, I didn't stop reading just 'cause school was over. I remembered what y'all said about how reading helps you learn. Looks like I learned a lot this summer 'cause I read five books."

Discovering Diamonds in the Rough

Though improving students' literacy skills is a starting point, it is by no means the only way to turn low performers into high achievers. As a team, we also have to show students *how* to learn. This might seem obvious, even disingenuous, but the truth is that many young adolescents do not understand how to "do" school. They don't know why some students seem to get the game while others don't. It's as if they were absent the day the rules were explained.

When working with the Challenge program, for example, we quickly discovered that our struggling students were extremely curious, articulate, introspective, and interested in learning. They craved success, yet they continuously came up short because they didn't know how to demonstrate their knowledge and skills, at least in conventional terms. Not surprisingly, the students were distrustful of teachers and administrators and considered school an unpleasant place. We had to show them a different side.

We started with positive self-talk. Steven was typical of the students on the Challenge team. He believed he was "stupid," a "failure," a boy who belonged at the back of the class. Standardized tests made him particularly anxious. The upcoming end-of-year test would determine whether or not he would advance to high school, and Steven was terrified of failing.

At the end of each day during the week the state set aside for annual testing, Steven would come to us dejected and unsure. We would give him a team pep talk. "You can do this," we told him. "You have worked so hard. Look at how much better your reading abilities are than they were in the beginning. You are ready."

Each morning we would urge him on with similar phrases, and Steven would trudge through another day of testing. He would thank us for believing in him commenting, "Y'all really make me feel like I can do this." During lunch we actually overheard Steven commenting to another student about the test, "Sure, man, you can do it. Just believe in yourself."

Other times we pulled students outside to discuss their strengths: "John, you are such a leader in our class. Your opinion is valued by the other students, especially Sam. I don't want Sam to know this, but I need help. Is there any way you could just mention things like, 'Sam, you are really good in math,' or ask Sam to 'help' you with something?"

This approach serves two purposes. First, it draws out students' natural talents. John began guiding the class in a positive direction. Second, students hear positive comments from someone other than their teachers. Sam needed to know that his peers thought well of him.

The one pitfall to avoid when modeling positive talk is fake praise. You have to be sincere, or kids will eat you alive. In addition, the praise can't be the same for every student. It must be specific and address individual needs. Over time, students start internalizing the positive messages. What they hear becomes what they think about themselves. We experienced this professionally as well. When we were preparing our presentation for the Disney Teacher Awards, we felt as scared and unsure as many of our students do on test days. We'll never forget the pep talk that Steven provided.

"You can do this," he told us one morning. "You have worked so hard; just show them what ya got. Isn't that what you told me? If it works for me, shouldn't it work for you?"

Visualizing Success

We realize that we won't always be around to give our students the moral support they need to tackle tough tasks, so we teach them to use their talents to overcome their weaknesses. Some of our students find it quite difficult to acknowledge their strengths, so we systematically help them identify what they do well so they can rely on their strengths in difficult situations.

To uncover students' talents, particularly the talents of those with learning disabilities, it helps to work collaboratively with your colleagues. We're not proud to admit this, but in the past we often viewed our special education students through a different lens than our "regular" students. Before Kathryn joined our team, we often fell into the habit of creating different, less difficult versions of class work for our special needs students. Our perception was that they could not pass our classes if they were required to do the same activities we'd planned for our general population students. Kathryn's presence on our team challenged us to plan our lessons so that our special needs students received strategies and individualized support to help them complete the same class work required for other students.

Terrence was one student who opened our eyes. In math class one afternoon, we asked students to work with partners and use graph paper and string to solve a fixed-area problem based on the famous feud between the Hatfields and McCoys.

As our students were trying to figure out how much fence Mr. Hatfield would need to separate his pigs from Mr. McCoy's field, Terrence suddenly jumped up and shouted, "Hey! Make it a square. That's it!"

Amanda was so surprised she jumped back. Terrence was usually a quiet, almost withdrawn student who seldom had the correct answer. When Amanda asked him to explain his reasoning by writing it on the whiteboard, he confidently elaborated for the other students.

"Y'all look at this," he said. "If I make my string into a square, I have more area with the same perimeter. Now that is cool."

His peers stared at him, not sure whether they should believe him. Terrence dismissed them with an insouciant wave of his hand. "I'm right," he declared and strutted back to his seat.

Amanda asked him later how he came up with the answer so quickly, and he replied, "I dunno, but I just saw it in my head somehow."

How often do we present lessons or accept answers only one way in our classrooms? What would happen if we periodically shifted the perspective, as one might do by turning a kaleidoscope to get an alternate view? Could we help students like Terrence suddenly see the light? Teamwork encouraged us to ask ourselves such questions, and collaboration enabled us to find some new solutions.

In our daily consultations and planning with Kathryn, we examined Terrence's math breakthrough through a metacognitive lens: *how* had he learned about learning? Initially, it seemed that while his brain was processing new information, he did not understand what to do with the data. His inability to *see* concepts and connect them to prior knowledge had slowed him down. That is, until the day he found the right tools.

Roger Farr (2002) further clarified this for us during a presentation at National Middle School Association's annual conference. Farr suggested that many students do not realize they are supposed to be thinking as they look at the words on a page. As a result, they may recall words later but not comprehend them.

After we returned to school following the conference, we discussed how the inability to think about their learning might have handicapped some of our students. Amanda recalled those who weren't able to visualize word problems in math, even when she asked them to draw the equations. Amanda and Monique then began compiling and comparing lists of students who didn't seem to have a cognitive compass, and the overlap from subject to subject was astounding. We knew we had to make some changes in our instruction.

We started by consciously crafting lessons designed to make the learning process more transparent. We constructed our worksheets so they focused on students' thought processes rather than following a traditional fill-in-the-blank format. For example, we developed reading guides such as the one shown in Figure 4.1.

Such guides not only improve reading comprehension and math problem-solving skills, they also help us monitor students and correct any misperceptions. As students read silently, we can walk around the classroom and observe their illustrations and comments on the reading guides. Based on what we see, we can quietly redirect a student or make a notation to conduct a mini-lesson later for several students without interrupting the current activity. During our walk-arounds, Kathryn asks the special education students to explain the reading guide to her in order to check for comprehension in addition to tracking their pace through the story.

Visualization guides used in all subject areas eventually double as guides for our large-group discussions, which we call share circles. Because we know that students are more apt to internalize information they actively discuss, all of us use focused classroom conversations to extend our instruction. However,

"The Lady or the Tiger" Reading Guide

Directions: As you read the story "The Lady or the Tiger," each time you come to an asterisk (*) that I have placed within the text, pause and reflect upon what you've read so far. Then fill in the chart for the section you've just completed reading.

Draw a picture of what happened	What questions do you have?	What do you predict will happen next?
*1)		
*2)		
*3)		

What do you think happens after this story ends?

What is the effect of this surprise ending on the reader?

What do you want to discuss with the class?

Figure 4.1 "The Lady or the Tiger" Reading Guide

in the past we were often disappointed by the results because our students were not discussing topics with any depth or sharing information with each other. Instead, they waited for us to prompt them and tried to give us the answers they thought we were searching for. Or they let one or two of their peers supply all the answers while the rest took notes and remained silent.

A typical exchange went like this: After reading "If I Had a Country, I Should Be a Patriot" by Frederick Douglass (1847), "Ain't I a Woman" by Sojourner Truth (1851), and "Sympathy" by Paul Laurence Dunbar (1899), students answered some questions individually; then we talked about the literature.

Monique: *What does the bird in this poem symbolize?*

Dakota: *Slaves.*

Monique: *How do you know it's about slaves?*

Samantha: *They're trying to get free and they're being held against their will. It says they keep beating against the bars of the cage.*

Monique: *How does this poem relate to what we've been studying in history and the two speeches we've read?*

[Silence]

Monique: *Anyone?*

[Silence]

Monique: *Think about what we've been studying.*

George: *It's about slavery and going free.*

Monique: *Yes, Morgan?*

Morgan: *What's the answer to number 3?*

Obviously, this was not the stimulating and enlightening conversation we had intended. We complained about these lopsided dialogues during our team meetings, but initially we didn't know how to improve them. Through ongoing discussions, research, and observations, we realized that just as students needed to be taught how to think about what they were reading, they needed direct instruction about how to talk about what they were learning.

We started by arranging our classrooms in a circle for discussions. Facing each other encouraged students to respond to the person who had spoken last. We asked students to address one another by name. When students directed their responses to us instead of to the speaker, we remained silent.

This was difficult to do in the early stages, but by refusing to make meaning for students we helped them learn how to do so themselves. Tentatively at first, and then more confidently, they offered responses to one another. Later, we rejoined the conversations to redirect topics or to clarify misconceptions.

We discovered that before they could discuss topics in depth, many students needed time to gather their thoughts and practice phrasing substantive questions and responses. Small groups provided a safe training space. Using discussion guides, students would work with several peers to analyze a topic and prepare follow-up questions for larger class discussions. Kathryn would pull some of the groups aside to review the discussion guide and let the students practice their questioning and answering techniques so they might feel more confident when addressing their classmates. This method proved especially helpful to our special needs students, whose language processing delays inhibited their oral discourse. Figure 4.2 includes a discussion guide we prepared for the literature series previously mentioned.

Because they had adequate "think time" and the chance to try out their ideas on a smaller audience, students became more confident presenting their ideas to the whole class. Now our classroom conversations are much richer and more nuanced than before. Consider the difference in this recent discussion about the Douglass, Truth, and Dunbar essays:

Monique: *Over the course of the last three days we've read "Ain't I a Woman" by Sojourner Truth, "If I Had a Country, I Should Be a Patriot" by Frederick Douglass, and "Sympathy" by Paul Laurence Dunbar. I'd like to discuss those three pieces of writing. Who'd like to start?*

Tyler: *The poem is deep as in deep like sad and emotional. I thought this because it says the bird is bleeding on the cruel bars. It makes it sound sad and deep.*

Discussion Guide for "If I Had a Country, I Should Be a Patriot," "Ain't I a Woman," and "Sympathy"

1. What common themes can you find in these three pieces?

2. Douglass claimed that a true patriot is one who "rebukes and does not excuse its (the country's) sins." How does this apply to your responsibilities as a citizen?

3. Sojourner Truth was a black woman and therefore was denied many rights in the 1800s. What is the most important right that she was denied? Why do you think so?

4. What similarities exist among Frederick Douglass, Sojourner Truth, and the caged bird?

5. Can freedom exist without people being willing to fight for it?

6. List three questions or topics that you'd like to discuss with the entire class.

Figure 4.2 Sample Discussion Guide

Dustin: *I agree with you, Tyler, because it [the bird] is representing slavery. It makes you think of how slaves were beaten and hurt and how they prayed. It's sad.*

Monique: *So, Dustin says the bird represents a slave. What do we call that in literature when something represents something else?*

Amanda and Ariana: *Symbolism.*

Monique: *Knowing this is symbolism, what do you think of Tyler's comment about the wings beating against the bars of the cage?*

Tyler: *I think the wings are like the whip.*

Jude: *Well, no, I think when his wings are beating against the bars it's like he's trying to get free, but every time he tries to it would just get worse. Then he'd bleed more and fly back to his perch until he was strong enough to try it again.*

Monique: *Ahhh . . . until he was strong enough to try again. So, Tyler says it reminds him of the whip; Jude says it's representing looking for freedom. Let's go with the freedom thought for a minute. Does freedom mean something? Anyone?*

Joseph: *It should. You should respect it. It's a privilege, not a right.*

Tyler and Donovan: *It is actually a right.*

At this point many students boisterously jumped in with their opinions and continued the conversation, debating whether freedom is guaranteed by the Constitution.

The mundane question-and-answer sessions of the past have been replaced by these engaging discussions, thanks to deliberate instruction about the art of conversation and guided reflection time to articulate ideas.

Stimulating the Brain

All this thinking about thinking led to the creation of a short multidisciplinary unit focused on the human brain. Using resources such as David Sousa's *How the Brain Learns* (2005b) and *How the Brain Learns to Read* (2005a) and Robert Sylwester's *How to Explain a Brain* (2005), we wove mini-lessons about metacognition into our daily curriculum.

For example, in science class, Amanda developed a sequence on the brain's physiology. She discussed the proper care of the brain, including sleep and exercise needs. In math class, she asked students to chart their sleep patterns for one week. We were shocked to discover that 85 percent of our students were getting less than four hours of sleep per night, when the recommended time for young adolescents is eight and a quarter to nine and a half hours a night (Breus 2004). Amanda challenged students to adjust their sleep habits to reach the recommended level for one week and write about their emotional and physical responses in their dialogue journals.

April's comments were indicative of the profound insights students gained as a result of their studies. "I thought I was depressed and dumb," she wrote. "I just needed sleep." Her grades improved sharply after she began sleeping eight hours a night.

As part of our unit on the brain, Monique taught mini-lessons in reading about how the brain reads and what is supposed to be happening. To help students understand, Monique used a filing cabinet analogy to illustrate how the brain stores and retrieves schema, thus allowing us to connect new information to what we've previously learned.

The students began to vocalize the connections they were making while they read. "Hey, Mrs. Wild, this passage reminds me of last year when we visited the beach with my grandparents. Is that a schema connection?" In this way the brain focus was revisited periodically throughout the year by us and by the students. Many students were so intrigued that they joined the website Neuroscience for Kids at http://faculty.washington.edu/chudler/neurok.html.

The knowledge students gained about their learning habits helped them become less dependent on us and showed them how much they could contribute to their education. The brain and metacognition unit was especially helpful for the special education students as they learned to associate new knowledge with prior knowledge using the "brain-as-a-filing-cabinet" metaphor. As a result, we started encouraging them to set specific and measurable academic goals. Vague ambitions, such as "I will do better in reading class," were unacceptable. Rather, we pushed for real progress: "I will read at least twenty pages a night of a grade-level (or higher) book to increase my fluency and vocabulary." Learning how to analyze students' learning needs so they could achieve these goals became the next phase of our agenda.

We encouraged students to reflect on their previous struggles and identify some possible causes, such as poor study habits or weak organizational skills. With this information, we could help them design an intervention plan, including seeking help from teachers and peers and setting up self-incentives to improve motivation. For special education students, we helped them align their personal goals with the goals stated in their federal individualized education plan (IEP) documents. In turn, at their IEP conferences we could show their parents and the administrators what the students were working on to help themselves meet their yearly goals. Figure 4.3 shows one of the tools we developed for this purpose.

Throughout the school year, students reflect on their successes and failures and adjust their goals accordingly. They look at their test scores, class assignments and projects, report-card grades, and other evidence of achievement. They rate their classroom performance on a scale of 1–10 across all subject areas and also track their reading habits, visits to the disciplinarian's office, and their greatest accomplishments during each nine-week grading period. Figure 4.4 shows one of the self-evaluation tools we use.

Students also must provide detailed answers to the following questions:

1. What accomplishment achieved during this grading period are you most proud of? Why?
2. How many books have you read during this grading period? List them, and highlight your favorite.
3. What do you really need to improve? Why?
4. What specific things can you do to make this improvement?
5. What is the most important thing you have learned so far this year? Explain.

For added encouragement, we kept copies of all the goal sheets and self-evaluations to use whenever we met with students or their families. Students also strived to keep each other on course by sharing their goals and evaluations during peer conferences. These student-to-student coaching sessions became a regular part of our team repertoire when we realized how much structured support struggling students needed to reach their academic and behavioral targets.

We designed an academic success plan that included the following components:

Support Team

- All team members, both students and teachers, identified their strengths and weaknesses.
- We posted the list of identified strengths throughout the team areas.
- Students could use other team members' strengths to assist them with their own weaknesses.
- We provided time twice each week for peer tutors to help other students with academics.

Goals for _____ Grading Period

First Area of Concern: _____

Remember: Your goals should be very specific. You should be able to provide evidence that you have worked toward and reached your goals. Focus on small accomplishments that will assist you in achieving these important goals.

My goal is:

The reason I chose this goal is:

My three-step plan for achieving this goal is:

1. _____

2. _____

3. _____

Midterm
(when interim reports are sent home)

This is what I have done to work on my goal so far:

Check one:

_____This is what I still have to do:

_____I am making the following changes to my plan:

End of Grading Period

_____Yes, I accomplished my goal.

Provide proof:

_____No, I did not accomplish my goal because:

Figure 4.3 Forms to Help Students Set and Work Toward Self-Identified Academic Goals

Self-Evaluation
Third Grading Period

Subject	First Period Grade	Second Period Grade	Third Period Grade	Reflections: What changes do you notice in your work since the last grading period? What must you do in this subject in order to do better? (Be specific.)
Math				
Language Arts				
Science				
Social Studies				

Figure 4.4 Self-Evaluation Tool

Mentors

- We assigned student and teacher mentors to every student who was in danger of failing and scheduled regular times for them to meet.
- Teacher mentors kept detailed records of every child in danger of failing.
- Mentors were responsible for reminding assigned students to continue working toward their goals: "Jake, maybe you should be writing this down in your notebook."
- Students moved in and out of mentor groups according to individual needs.

After-School Assistance

- Free tutoring sessions (with classmates) were available twice a week after school.
- Students had to sign up for after-school sessions at least one day in advance.

Zero Alerts

- When any student failed to complete an assignment, we sent a notice home and required the student to attend scheduled after-school sessions.

Braggin' Rights

- We celebrated successes by noting each student's accomplishments on our team Braggin' Rights list. Often, students wrote about their classmates.

Surprisingly, the most difficult step in the plan was the first one. Although our students had no problem identifying their weaknesses, many struggled to identify their strengths. This was especially true of our special needs students. They were under the impression that they had nothing to offer the other students on the team. Their classmates quickly disproved that fallacy by pointing out their strengths:

"Amy, you are really good at presentations. You could help us practice ours."

"John, you run better than everyone in here. I could use some help in P.E. If you'd run beside me, I'd probably finish the mile next time."

Our students eventually began to barter with one another for assistance: "Stacy, I've never seen a planner or book sack as organized as yours. Could you help me clean out my binder, and I'll help you with math?"

Together, we learned how to use our collective strengths to overcome individual weaknesses. In hindsight, that sounds like a simple concept, but it represented a revolutionary event for our team, moving us from a group of people sharing a schedule to an integrated unit responsible for the success of all members.

As a result of our focus on goal setting and managing daily progress using the academic success plan, we saw large improvements in our students' academic performance. After the first grading period, 11 percent of core class grades were Fs. By the end of the third grading period, that number was down to 4 percent. By the fourth grading period, 32 percent of our students were on the honor roll, many for the first time. In addition, 29 percent of our students had improved in all subject areas.

The most significant data we can provide to illustrate the effects of our focus on developing students as learners occurred a year after we implemented the academic success plan. All of our students passed the state's annual high-stakes test. None of our students was retained.

One of our finest compliments came from Marvin's dad, who told us he had arranged to take his son on a fishing trip as a reward for making good grades. Marvin was the one who insisted that the trip occur on a weekend instead of during the school week. "He told me he was afraid he would miss something exciting," his dad said.

Part 2
Connected Content

If an unfriendly foreign power had attempted to impose on America the mediocre educational performance that exists today, we might well have viewed it as an act of war. As it stands, we have allowed this to happen to ourselves. We have even squandered the gains in student achievement made in the wake of the Sputnik challenge. Moreover, we have dismantled essential support systems which helped make those gains possible. We have, in effect, been committing an act of unthinking, unilateral educational disarmament.

A Nation at Risk, 1983

Educational standards became the battle cry for American schools almost twenty-five years ago, but change has moved slowly. Ideas formulated when Monique and Amanda were in middle school and Kathryn was barely walking are just now taking hold in our classrooms.

Whether or not we agree with all the policies and requirements, we are examining student performance like never before. Without the No Child Left Behind legislation, would districts be scrambling to reconfigure the school where only 25 percent of the students score at the proficient level? Would we concern ourselves with the persistently poor performance of certain student sub-groups? Until the standards and accountability movement forced us to reconsider some of our assumptions and practices, we were not. We glossed over outrageously high minority dropout rates or tragically low special education reading levels with data that celebrated more stellar students.

As a nation we are finally looking at the big picture. Public education's goal is no longer making sure that Mrs. Brown completes her Tuesday lesson plan for sixth-grade history. The goal is ensuring that all students have the knowledge and skills necessary to be innovative, reflective, and contributing members of a society that never stands still. Every teacher plays a crucial role in moving students along the educational continuum. Standards require us to know where our students have been, where they need to go, and where they will be when they leave our classrooms.

Without teamwork, we cannot prepare students to meet the challenges of the next millennium. If each teacher individually tries to address every curricular objective and cycle back to the broader standards of learning, there will never be enough time in the day or the school year to finish the job. We have to work together to integrate and reinforce important concepts from all subjects, teaching students that learning is recursive, related, and really, really cool.

ChapterFive
Cutting the Fluff

The standards are coming! The standards are coming! This revolutionary battle cry reached a fevered pitch in U.S. schools when the No Child Left Behind legislation took effect. The structure of American education was shifting rapidly. As teachers, we were not ready or eager for the new requirements. We were among those who fought to defend our educational freedom.

In the beginning, we viewed standards as coconspirators of standardized assessments that were robbing us of professional decision-making. Our defenses rose, and we spent a great deal of time resisting the inevitable. What we did not realize at the time was that our rebellion was rooted in our confusion about the new expectations and the impact they would have on our students. We could not fathom how specific content standards could unite our teaching practices or guide our instructional planning. As we struggled through the transition period to the standards era, our team meetings provided a forum for examining the mandates professionally and responsibly. In the process, we discovered that what we were holding onto so vehemently was comfort. The collaborative units we had designed prior to the standards movement were not as engaging or thought-provoking as we once believed.

Truthfully, when we started working together as a team, curriculum integration was more of an afterthought than a consistent way of teaching. We did not weave deeply connected lessons into our practices. We spent most of our time developing guiding concepts and establishing team procedures. After we became comfortable with collaborative teaching structures, we felt prepared to tackle the substance of curriculum integration.

Our initial attempts were superficial. A typical example occurred when Monique was teaching a unit on fantasy in literature and Amanda obligingly renamed all the characters in the math problems after the characters in the stories. There were no significant interdisciplinary connections to the curriculum objectives. The lessons were cute, often entertaining, but they provided little depth.

To create stronger interdisciplinary units, we knew we had to probe the subject content that each of us understood independently but not collaboratively. Then we had to link common themes and figure out a way to present them concurrently. That proved easier to think about than to do. Trying to establish meaningful connections across three or four subjects made us dizzy, so we started small and concentrated on connecting the curriculum objectives of two subjects at a time.

One year, for example, we became incensed by the traffic tie-ups near our school. Many cars exceeded the speed limit, and we were concerned about our students' safety. Searching for a way to link academics with activism, Amanda asked the students in her math classes to collect data about the speeders. Using beginning and end points and a stop watch, students calculated the drivers' average speed by using the formula, distance = rate x time.

After measuring the distance between a start point and end point, pairs of students timed how quickly each car covered the distance. Then they found the average speed of the cars passing in front of the school. Using the data, our students then wrote persuasive letters in language arts class to report their findings to local authorities and urge them to post additional patrol cars during high traffic periods.

This was a basic approach to curriculum integration, to be sure, but the success of such simple collaborations whetted our appetites for more. Over time we were able to involve all core teachers in most interdisciplinary units; yet involving every teacher physically and academically still wasn't enough to raise the interdisciplinary lessons to the level of excellence.

Consider the integrated unit that we developed and called "the living history museum." According to the standards for eighth-grade language arts, students had to learn how to write research papers. To reinforce historical concepts included in the social studies benchmarks, we decided to base the research assignment on historical figures from the first half of the twentieth century. After they completed their research papers, students turned every classroom on the team into a museum, each representing a different decade. Throughout the day, students dressed and acted the parts of the people they'd researched while other students and invited guests toured the museum.

Although this unit addressed only the social studies and language arts objectives, it involved all the teachers on the team, so we thought we had successfully integrated the curriculum. Yet, we still had more work to do.

Looking Beneath the Surface

In 2005, when our district adopted the Louisiana Comprehensive Curriculum, which outlined what students had to learn in each subject and the specific weeks in which we had to teach those concepts, our jobs became more challenging. However, ironically, the inflexible curriculum helped us see the wisdom of making our lessons more tightly focused and connected.

The standards addressed in our curriculum documents provided a clear indication of what our students should be able to do as a result of their educational experiences. We could no longer hide behind fluffy activities with vague intentions. If we wanted to successfully address our individual class requirements while simultaneously showing students how the ideas from one course applied to all the others, we had to truly understand those connections ourselves.

No, we don't carry around laminated curriculum cheat sheets to guide us (although, come to think of it, that might be a good project to consider for the future). Rather, our cross-curricular knowledge is the result of extensive mapping done prior to the beginning of each school year.

Heidi Hayes Jacobs defines curriculum mapping as a "procedure for collecting data about the operational curriculum in a school or district referenced directly to the calendar" (2004, 1). According to Jacobs, three types of information should be collected on a curriculum map. These include descriptions of content, descriptions of processes or skills to be emphasized, and assessment and expected student outcomes. We have discovered that placing this pertinent information about our individual curriculum requirements on a single document indicating the time frame in which curriculum requirements will be taught lets us view our students' academic year at a glance. By using our curriculum map, we are able to see a road map of the year we will spend with our students.

Although Jacobs offers many reasons why curriculum mapping is beneficial to teachers, schools, and school districts, our team's main purpose for mapping is to uncover the potential for creating integrated instructional units. Curriculum mapping made sense to us because we saw it as a way to view all of our requirements at one time. The move to curriculum mapping was a natural process in our shift from individual teachers focused on specific subject areas to a team of teachers working together to teach students what they need to know.

Jacobs points out that "by perusing the maps for potential linkages among subject matter, teachers discover possibilities for interdisciplinary units of study. Whether the focus is a topic, theme, issue or problem-based study, elementary and secondary teachers can use maps to find natural connections that will expand and underscore students' learning" (1997, 20).

Our curriculum mapping sessions usually take place in one of our homes during the summer break. Many teachers may argue that summer vacations should not be invaded with schoolwork, and certainly we'd prefer to be paid for the planning. But the process is so valuable and saves us so much time during the school year that we think it's worth the effort, no matter how intangible the payoff.

We sit at Monique's dining-room table, spread out our curriculum documents and oversized calendars, and pencil in the time frames for each unit that we plan to teach in each subject. We use colored sticky notes and markers to indicate the progression of topics for the various subjects. After roughing out this disconnected timeline, we start searching for obvious interdisciplinary links. For example, if students will be focusing on genetics and heredity in science at the same time that they'll be exploring probability in math, we quickly coordinate lessons within these two subjects and develop an integrated unit. If the language arts unit on nonfiction dovetails with the Civil War unit in history, students can read and analyze the Gettysburg Address and several speeches by abolitionist speakers.

Unfortunately, the majority of our school weeks are not set up for such easy integration, so we have to dig deeper. Sometimes we can shift the schedule and the order of the units from our rough draft. Other times we must look at what one teacher will already have covered and what another teacher may have coming up on the calendar and design an integrated unit that links the new knowledge to previous knowledge.

We indicate integration possibilities on our curriculum map calendar by highlighting the dates and units, using different colors to show connections. Then we search for similarities in the state standards that we are responsible for addressing in our respective classes. The state standards are different for every subject area, but they are based on a core set of learning experiences, which include communication, problem-solving, resource access and utilization, general knowledge, and citizenship. The global concepts represented in the standards are similar for all grade levels, but the skills students are expected to gain are reflected in different benchmarks for each subject and grade level.

As we identify overlapping standards, we list them in a separate area and build a list of possible interdisciplinary topics. On our team, language arts has become the hub for integrating activities. It is usually easy for Monique to think of literature that relates to the content in other classes. However, each of us contributes to the integration. All of us read widely and have a pack rat's habit of collecting information about a variety of topics.

Our conversations inspire other connections. The giant unit, described in the Introduction, resulted from one brainstorming session. We started the team meeting by focusing on our frustrations with four separate curricular strands that seemed abstract and unrelated. Rather than waste time with what a friend refers to as the three Gs of teaching—gripe, grandstand, and gossip—we searched for unifying themes that could connect our lessons.

Monique had begun the school year teaching fantasy, the required literary genre for the first grading period, but certainly not one of her favorites. She was thinking aloud about how she could introduce the story plots as well as teach students about metaphors and similes when Amanda suggested using fairy tales or comparing the real tales to popular Disney versions. That led to a long discussion about how language and stories evolve. We reached a dead end with our integration agenda that day, but the next morning we factored the curriculum requirements for history and mathematics into our team conversation. Erin was supposed to start teaching the American Revolution in history, and Amanda had to focus on ratio and proportion in mathematics. The previous year, Amanda had used a math problem that involved a giant, so she mentioned it.

This led to a quick connection to "Jack and the Beanstalk," and our giant unit suddenly had legs. Amanda, by her own admission, is obsessed with helping students understand that our country's founding was a pivotal point in human history. Some of us had recently seen the movie *The Patriot*, so we bantered about a David versus Goliath theme. Our synapses really fired then, and we were able to fill out the framework. What could have been an unproductive misery-loves-company session spiraled into one of our most effective collaborative teaching endeavors.

Because we know we may come across various sources to help us with our collaborative planning as time goes by, we do not make our final plans for integration during the curriculum mapping sessions. Instead, we use this time to preview the possibilities for the school year. Periodically, we pull out the calendar containing our map to review and revise our plans, making notes along the way so that when we meet again the following summer we will have the benefit of our previous experiences on which to build.

Interdisciplinary planning encourages you to eliminate sacred cows. Anyone on the team is entitled to offer ideas and feedback about any part of the curriculum. Amanda is comfortable espousing the key themes of the

American Revolution unit. Monique might insist that metaphors have a place in math problems. Kathryn reminds us to incorporate multisensory learning.

We also agree that learning is a recursive process and that our students benefit from revisiting topics throughout the year. Completing a unit that focused on certain themes does not put those topics out of play in the future. If we come across a related magazine or newspaper article, we don't file the information until next year. We interject these items into our current class activities and show students how what they previously learned relates to the real world.

Integration Gets Messy

During one of our curriculum mapping sessions to deal with the new state standards, we realized, to our horror, that our integrated units could no longer be neatly packaged and planned weeks in advance. If we intended to integrate, we would have to move in and out of each other's territory as the various curricula allowed.

We refer to this period as the beginning of our messy integration. One of our creations focused on Martians. Monique was in the midst of a science fiction unit, and in science the students were studying adaptations and survival, so we saw possibilities for collaboration. Unfortunately math was not easy to integrate with these themes, so Amanda only joined us for two days. As uncomfortable as this felt, we decided that we must allow the core classes to flow in and out of the unit naturally. We found comfort in the work of Jacobs, who points out that "interdisciplinary designs are best when sensible, not strained, integration is planned" and that "not all disciplines need to be involved in the lesson design of a unit" (1997, 21). If we had forced the connections, we would have created artificial lessons to justify a contrived theme.

Admittedly, the Martian unit that was about to descend on our students was a gimmick born of our frustration with how to integrate the curriculum when we could not see any clear or meaningful connections. Once again, we had to start small, this time within the state standards' stricter parameters.

When the Martians invaded our classrooms, we literally had our fingers crossed that the unit would make sense for our students. Being good, loyal team members, we leaped off the cliff together as we tried to messily link what we considered quite unrelated information.

"Tomorrow the invasion begins!" read the notes on the whiteboards in our classrooms. Our students buzzed with questions about the message's meaning, but we offered no clues. In the midst of her science fiction unit, Monique had found a wonderful Web-based article about a boy who had played the 1980s computer game, Space Invaders, using only his mind. The article linked to a video clip of the boy performing the extraordinary task (http://news-info.wustl.edu/news/page/normal/7800.html).

The unit's goal was to show students the relevance of science fiction to scientific inquiry and advancement, so Monique seized the moment. After students read the article, viewed the demonstration, and discussed the scientific implications, Monique gave them a few minutes to play online versions of Space Invaders. These few minutes of fun provided the hook for the brief thematic integration we had planned.

The next morning the message on our classroom whiteboards changed to "The Martians have landed!" Students gathered around the computer as though it were an old-fashioned radio and listened to the original *War of the Worlds* broadcast. Orson Wells began to spread terror just as he had on that fateful day of October 30, 1938. To reenact the drama, Monique and her students dramatized the scenes as the actors read the script. After the story ended, students were shocked to discover that in 1938 the broadcast had caused widespread panic.

"Oh, man, that's stupid!" some shouted. "They must have been easy to fool."

One of our students, Dylan, brought them back to reality. "Hey," he admitted, "I thought it was real for a minute."

Monique pointed out how different the students' lives were from those who first heard the broadcast seventy years ago. The discussion turned to how people's fears could be easily aroused, particularly when they depended on a single source for news.

"They did not have all of the stuff we have today," Cole said thoughtfully.

"What stuff?" asked Ann.

"Well, we have Internet, TV with twenty-four-hour news, and we have cell phones and all kinds of other stuff," Cole said.

"So I guess you could be tricked if all you had was a radio and you did not hear the first part of the broadcast," concluded Joey.

While the students were at lunch that day, the message on the classroom whiteboards changed to "Mission to Mars begins tomorrow." The students were excited and wanted to know how we planned to respond to the "alien invasion," but we let them go home for the day with more mysteries to be revealed.

The next morning, the students discovered that their teachers had been transformed into Martians. Green T-shirts, black pants, colorful makeup, and homemade antennae completed our costumes, while space-age music and a few decorations turned our classrooms into rocket ships ready to blast off into the great beyond.

When students from other teams asked what was going on, our students nonchalantly replied, "That's just our teachers; they do stuff like that all the time. It means we're doing something all together today." Yet their excitement grew as they began discussing the possible connections to their previous lessons.

Suddenly, Kathryn interrupted the conversations with a message that resonated over the P.A. system: "Attention, Flying Pigs. Yesterday, Martians invaded Earth. Today we are looking for the best of our team to complete a mission to Mars. Prepare for training. The astronauts we choose must meet very specific criteria. You will be informed of your duties to fulfill this mission. Remain on alert."

In math, Amanda had been ready to begin a unit on linear functions when a preassessment revealed that students had little understanding of a coordinate plane, a key step in the process. The students were fairly confident about using quadrant 1 of the coordinate plane but could not use a four-coordinate plane. So Amanda decided to backtrack. Our Martian integration provided a perfect context for pausing to assist students with concepts they needed to complete more advanced mathematical problems.

After a few activities designed to check for understanding, we asked the students to find partners for a game of Alien Invaders, Amanda's version of the popular board game Battleship. Amanda drew coordinate planes on large sheets of paper and laminated them. Each student received five different sizes of spaceships to place on their grids. The students played the game just like Battleship, using strategy to locate and destroy their opponents' spaceships.

Amanda and Kathryn circulated around the room, listening for correct coordinate directions. They watched as students who had previously struggled to understand the concepts or who had shown little interest in math began to seek the proper techniques so they could win the game. As students continued playing, Amanda and Kathryn pulled aside one or two students at a time to provide supplemental instruction.

Meanwhile, in science, students were moving into a unit about adaptation and survival of the fittest. Erin decided that the Martian activity would be a great hook. The adaptation activities took place in all of our classrooms rather than just the science room. We flexed our class schedules so we could have enough time at the end of the day for a Martian obstacle course. Students who had successfully completed all the activities would become the elite members of our colonization team, which would be sent to Mars to make peace with the Martians. In each class students completed several different tasks to see who had the necessary adaptations to survive a Martian voyage. The students rotated to a new station every few minutes.

In one classroom, students were greeted with the message, "Your mission to Mars requires you to follow a very specific flight pattern. To do so, you must be able to accurately lock in the coordinates for your flight. The following is a timed test. You must plot your flight course by decoding the message contained in your folders using the coordinate grid. You may begin." And so our students returned to the coordinate grid to reinforce the knowledge they'd gained earlier in Amanda's classroom.

At the next station, students were required to drink from a cup without using hands and without spilling any water. The message greeting these students was "The flight to Mars is a lengthy one. You must be able to drink water while confined in a very small space pod. To actually join the Mars crew, you must be able to demonstrate the ability to drink without the use of hands, and you may not spill. Spilled water will result in equipment malfunction within your space pods." So our students, through their laughter, attempted to drink without spilling.

In a third classroom, students had to meet a test of physical ability to perform a safety maneuver on the trip to Mars. In this station, we asked the students to stand flat-footed and touch a button taped to the wall with their hands. This task proved difficult for our shorter students, and the taller students felt superior and safe in their ability to make the trip to Mars. However, when the second physical test was introduced, our taller students groaned. They were now required to crawl through a small tunnel on their hands and knees and could not slide through on their bellies. Our smaller students now felt supreme and giggled hysterically as their physically imposing peers tried to fit through the tight space.

At the end of the day, nine students had completed all the tasks successfully. We met outside in our team commons area to officially welcome them as astronauts. The other students applauded the efforts, we presented the achievers with honorary Martian antennae, and our two-day integration was complete. However, the learning that was triggered by a shared experience continued.

Because of the limitations they had personally experienced in the unfamiliar "space" environment, our students could confidently discuss adaptations in nature during science class. Many noted that they would not have survived the space voyage based on the different standards of life on a spaceship bound for Mars.

In language arts, Monique continued with the science fiction unit for several more weeks. The rest of us returned to other requirements. Although the Martian invasion was a small interdisciplinary unit, it enabled us to capture our students' curiosity while showing them clear connections among different subjects.

Back to the Drawing Board

In retrospect, however, the unit could have been so much better. We used a cute theme, the Martians, for the pizzazz it would bring to our classrooms, but we should have stressed the underlying curriculum concepts from the beginning. Reflecting on our work helped us see how we could deepen the subject content and the interdisciplinary connections.

We turned to our individual curriculum documents for direction about the information and skills our students were expected to master. This led us to the next logical step: starting our collaborative planning by identifying the objectives—known as grade-level expectations—that our interdisciplinary units would address. We needed to take this step before we branched out to the activities and assessments that would help students meet those objectives. As a result, our collaborative conversations focused much more on the "why" of something we were doing with students instead of just the "what" and "how."

Erin entered our team meeting one day and said, "Okay, I have to teach about the Barbary Coast pirates. The [history] content standard says, 'Students will develop an understanding of fundamental economic concepts as they apply to the interdependence and decision-making of individuals, households, businesses, and governments in the United States and the world.' The benchmark requires me to show students how the pirates affected the economic systems in the world during the 1800s. I mean, doesn't that sound boring? How can we integrate this to generate interest? Can we make this relevant to their lives now? What do y'all have to teach right now?"

By posing those questions, Erin initiated another collaborative learning adventure. The following dialogue demonstrates how we learned to construct an interdisciplinary unit, working back and forth between the state standards and the curriculum objectives and reinforcing this foundation with engaging, relevant activities and assessments.

"Yikes," said Monique. "I'm teaching the research paper. I have to expose them to research methods, teach them how to write a bibliography, and stuff like that. We've already picked topics to match their science projects. This might be a hard one to integrate, but we should be able to do something, especially with [the movie] *Pirates of the Caribbean* being so popular."

"In math we're creating scatter plots," Amanda added, "but I've got a lesson that I usually teach with learning stations. I could make those stations match a pirate theme. Actually, that would work really well."

"Didn't I just see a news report about pirates attacking a cruise ship?" asked Kathryn.

Erin thought about this for moment. "Yeah, could we do something with modern pirates, too?" she asked.

Christine Wood, a paraprofessional who works with our team, was busy researching on the computer. "Here's an article about the ship attack, and there's a bunch of stuff about digital piracy," she said.

"Oooooo," Monique said, squealing with delight. "I could teach them to research using the Internet, and we could gather information on digital piracy. Amanda, could you graph the data we collect? Does that go with scatter plots? Erin, don't you have a [content] benchmark about collecting data, too? We could reference the sites using bibliography entries. That would give us the opportunity to practice a bit before we go in search of information about their science topics. Finding information about piracy might help them realize why we actually use bibliographies."

Erin quickly delegated responsibilities. "Monique and Kathryn, I need to get some input on a possible reading guide for the Barbary Coast pirate information," she said. "I'd like them to gather information using the book. If I helped them see how to use the parts of the book to find information, would that go with your research stuff? Could y'all help me come up with a guide that will teach them a reading strategy?"

Initially, our core curriculum units seemed very disconnected, but the lack of obvious similarities failed to dissuade us. We didn't stop to think about whether we *could* relate these units of study; we just figured out how we *would*.

The following week, our students entered the team area and found us dressed in pirate costumes. The soundtrack to *Pirates of the Caribbean* blared through the classrooms.

"So, ye want to join my crew?" Amanda asked the bemused students, using her best pirate imitation. "Well, ye landlubbers, you better know something about the x- and y-axis. Who can tell me what slope is? And if ye get it wrong, ye walk the plank!"

Laughing and intrigued, the adolescent crew members quickly assembled to begin the voyage. The mathematics ship then set sail to find treasures hidden in scatter plots.

For this unit, Amanda referred not only to the district curriculum documents but also to the National Council of Teachers of Mathematics, whose standards for middle grades students expect that they will be able to:

- represent, analyze, and generalize a variety of patterns, tables, graphs, words, and, when possible, symbolic rules
- relate and compare different forms of representation for a relationship
- identify functions as linear or nonlinear and contrast their properties from tables, graphs, or equations (2000)

Amanda and Kathryn next set up seven learning stations with different activities designed to allow students to discover algebraic relationships through simulations. Each student received a "ship log" to record data and answer questions, such as the following: What is the independent variable? What is the dependent variable? Is your graph positive, negative, or no correlation?

At each station the directions were written in pirate lingo and consisted of common activities such as seeing the distance a toy car travels depending on the height of the ramp or the width of a water drop depending on the height of the dropper.

Rotating every fifteen minutes through the learning stations, students completed all the math activities in two days. Afterward, we conducted a group discussion to clear up any questions and misconceptions. These activities provided a strong introduction to algebraic thinking.

Next, we related nineteenth-century piracy to the twenty-first century by asking students to collect opinion surveys about the recent practice of downloading music from the Internet without paying writers and musicians. We made the assignment in science class to address the state standard for gathering and organizing data, but we asked students to submit their work in language arts class as part of their research about Internet piracy.

After compiling the data, students completed a Web Quest, which is an inquiry tool teachers can use to guide students to appropriate online resources for specific technology-based projects. (You may learn more about Web Quests at http://webquest.org.) The piracy Web Quest required students to define historical, digital, and Internet piracy and cite examples of each. Students compared the definitions of Internet and digital piracy to their peers' perceptions about copying and downloading music, based on the surveys. Then they created online posters using Web Poster Wizard (http://poster.4teachers.org/index.php) and properly cited the graphic and text sources reflected in their presentations.

"Ahhh," said Tate, as a virtual lightbulb illuminated his brain. "If we don't put these bibliographies on our posters, we are actually pirates, aren't we?"

Suddenly bibliographic entries had a real purpose.

We made relevant connections to other subject content as well. Instead of asking students to read the history textbook's explanation of the Barbary Coast pirates and answer some questions at the end of the chapter, Erin let the students dramatize key events and use reading guides as they gathered information for a class debate. Topic: Were the Barbary Coast pirates harmful or helpful to the United States economy?

Each of the teachers on the team could have met the curriculum objectives independently, but by collaborating, we set the stage for deeper learning that lingered long after the pirates had vanished from school. Five months after we had completed the unit, DeAundré rushed into the team area and shouted, "Pull up the Web. I gotta show you this site where I saw that there is a bounty on dogs that can sniff out music piracy."

How's that for evidence of the lasting impact of curriculum integration?

More Fine-Tuning

Although the pirate unit showed us how much stronger integration could be when we used the curriculum objectives as our starting point, we still were not satisfied with our efforts. We were continuing to use themes to connect standards and skills in a contrived way. We were not really demonstrating for students how math, science, history, English, and other subjects consistently related. We had to do a better job of identifying and reflecting the connected, global concepts during our team planning.

What do middle grades students need to know and be able to do to become productive and compassionate adults who can confidently navigate an ever-changing world? By repeatedly reflecting on this question, we have realized that our main purpose as an interdisciplinary team must be modeling and teaching students *how* to learn. We can't possibly share every idea and skill they'll need in the future. We don't know what the world will look like in ten years, twenty years, or for the rest of their lives. But we can give them the tools to find their way.

We can teach students to communicate effectively, to work productively, to treat others respectfully, to read critically, to persist through difficulty, and to lead democratically. These are not merely nice ambitions. They are the reasons we send children to school. And whether we are studying Greek mythology or the causes and consequences of pollution, we can frame our inquiries by asking the question students want and need to know: What does this have to do with me and the rest of the world?

Surprisingly, we found that most of the answers could be found in the state's academic standards. The realization that we did not have to fight the standards movement but could work within it to provide excellent educational opportunities for our students was liberating after all. When we reached this conclusion, we felt free to creatively and responsively address our students' needs, knowing that the standards would help us prepare them for high school, college, and careers.

ChapterSix
Unifying the Curriculum

The federal No Child Left Behind legislation turned our teaching upside down. The school standards and accountability movement forced us to change dramatically the way we made professional decisions within our classrooms.

When we began searching for global concepts to unify our lessons, we based our decisions on what we thought middle grades students should know. We listed the most important ideas, such as citizenship, and decided as a team how to teach these concepts to our students. Yet, however valid our opinions might have been, we could not satisfy the new accountability requirements with such limited justification.

We found the necessary rationale within the standards. Furthermore, the standards included benchmarks and grade-level expectations that told us exactly what students should be able to do to meet the broader learning goals. Here were the universal themes we had been seeking to link our interdisciplinary units: freedom, citizenship, and communication. And within our individual curriculum documents, we identified the topics and skills that would help us convey those ideas to our students.

For example, Louisiana's social studies standards for seventh grade indicate that students should "develop an understanding of the structure and purposes of government, the foundations of the American democratic system, and the role of the United States in the world while learning about the rights and responsibilities of citizenship"(Louisiana Administrative Code 2005). This standard articulated more clearly what we intended to communicate when we chose citizenship as an important global concept. Middle-level benchmarks associated with this citizenship standard in our social studies curriculum include the following:

1. Describe the essential characteristics of various systems of government.
2. Explain how the powers of government are distributed, shared, and limited by the United States Constitution.

3. Explain the meaning and importance of basic principles of the American Constitution.
4. Explain the meaning and importance of basic principles of American constitutional democracy as reflected in core documents.
5. Discuss issues involving the rights and responsibilities of individuals in American society.
6. Describe the many ways by which citizens can organize, monitor, and help to shape politics and government at local, state, and national levels.

After noting the expectations within each of our curricular strands, we worked with our teammates to find strong interdisciplinary connections so students would understand how a concept such as citizenship relates to all of their classes. We knew we would have to engage in long-term planning to make the cross-curricular links effective, so we began our collaborative implementation of the citizenship standard during the summer. First, we reviewed the benchmarks and discussed how they could be addressed in our individual classes. Figure 6.1 shows how we identified four of the six required language arts units in which the citizenship standard could be easily incorporated.

When we placed our individual ideas for integration on our team curriculum map, we realized that December would arrive before we would all be in a position to connect the information thematically in multiple subjects. This forced us, once again, to shift the way we thought about curriculum integration, moving farther away from those neat packages we had designed earlier in our collaboration. We knew we did not want our students to miss important connections for the sake of a beautiful, linear lesson plan, so we decided to weave the citizenship standard throughout the school year. We continually pointed out to students, "Hey, this is important. It's related to our citizenship theme."

Because we were still working collaboratively toward the same academic goal, we didn't feel pressured to make weak or artificial links just to satisfy our urge to integrate the curriculum. We waited until we could make clear and relevant connections. The best opportunity to combine our efforts came at the end of the second grading period. As is often the case, our creativity was inspired by a desire to meet our students' varied needs and a frank discussion of what had not worked in the past.

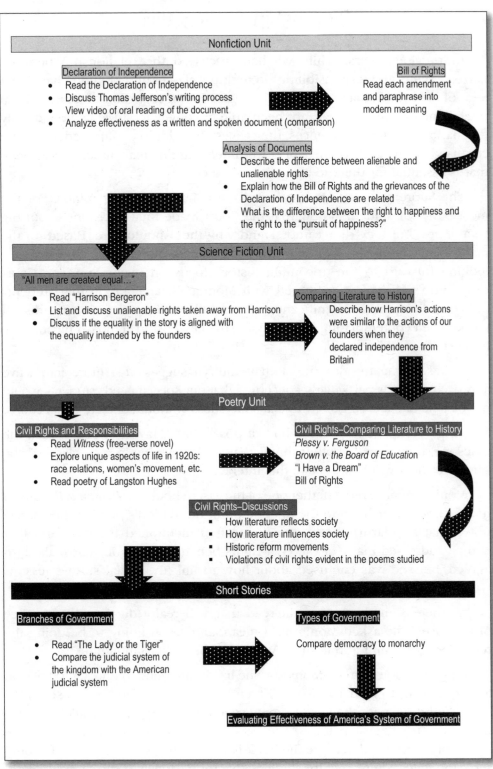

Figure 6.1 Language Arts Flow Chart Illustrating Incorporation of Curriculum Requirements with Identified Citizenship Standard Being Addressed by Our Team

Citizenship Comes Alive

In previous years, while we had discussed the relationship between citizens' rights and responsibilities in multiple classes and Monique had spent a lot of time in language arts examining the Bill of Rights and literature from the colonial period, we had not been able to convey to students how deeply the nation's history influences their lives. In addition, our students were confused about each branch of government's individual duties, knowledge that is essential for them to act as informed citizens.

The Supreme Court's role seemed most muddy in their minds. For the most part, our students knew that the Court made final decisions about big legal cases, but they didn't understand why they should care. Based on the many blank faces she had seen during previous discussions, Erin was not looking forward to the upcoming history focus on major Supreme Court cases. Erin's hesitation combined with Monique's lamentation that students didn't understand the significance of the Bill of Rights left us in a dismal mood when contemplating how to make the citizenship standard meaningful for seventh graders.

It was during this low point that Kathryn suggested a more interactive approach. She was particularly concerned that our special needs students would not be able to make sense of these abstract ideas without concrete connections.

Erin's response included a hint of possibility: "Maybe I need to pick the cases we study to match other things that are happening in your classes," she said. "But how would we make this interactive?"

Monique wondered whether one of the cases should be *Brown v. the Board of Education*, which led to the integration of our nation's public schools. She noted that standardized test questions often mentioned the case and that *Brown* addressed many of the civil rights benchmarks in our curricula. Erin agreed, but she was confused about how to link the social studies lessons with the language arts requirements.

"Is there something you can read that will really dig into the essence of the case?" she asked Monique. "I mean, aren't you going to be doing the required poetry unit at that time? Won't that be hard to integrate?"

Erin's question sparked Monique. She had been trying to find a good reason to ask students to read *Witness* by Karen Hesse (2001). The book is set in the 1920s and deals with themes of prejudice and the struggle for equality, which tied into our citizenship focus. The novel's themes also would reinforce the events of *Brown*. And because the book is written in poetic free verse, it would serve the state requirement for studying that form. However, the curriculum did not call for an additional novel study, so Monique was having trouble defending the choice in light of other requirements. After some discussion, we realized that because we were planning to integrate the citizenship unit throughout our classes, Monique could rationalize the additional novel study because it would address content standards for multiple subjects.

Next, we discussed how we could make the topics engaging for seventh graders. Erin suggested asking them to conduct mini–judicial reviews to find Bill of Rights violations within the court case. She thought this activity would help students understand how the Supreme Court consults the Constitution when resolving legal issues.

Our conversation turned to other possibilities for relating the novel and the court case to the Bill of Rights and to the math and science concepts that Amanda and Erin would be addressing. When Amanda noted that she'd be teaching probability as her next required topic, Monique became excited again. Following the required poetry unit was a short story unit. What a great opportunity to introduce Frank Stockton's "The Lady or the Tiger" (1884), which tells the story of a young man who dares to fall in love with a king's daughter and is put on trial where his fate is determined not by evidence but by probability. The story could help us link the Supreme Court unit to the math unit on probability.

After hearing the plot description of "The Lady or the Tiger," Erin suggested that we help students explore different characters' perspectives within other stories they'd be reading. In her science classes, she had been struggling to help students understand perspective to no avail.

"Middle school kids are so self-involved that they can't or won't see others' points of view as being valid or valuable," she said. "They need to understand how a perspective can skew the results of an experiment if a person is not careful to remain neutral and report only the facts. And in history they need to understand that a person's perspective can skew the historical evidence that they study."

Erin was delighted when Monique shared that *Witness*, the novel the students would be reading during the poetry unit, was divided into chapters, each told from a different character's perspective. Here was another skill that we could weave throughout our classes so our students would develop a clearer understanding of how perspectives can alter information and conclusions. The mood of our team meeting went from chilly to cheerful.

By this point, our conversation had revealed several strong integration possibilities for *Brown*, but we still had not figured out how to build students' interest in the landmark Supreme Court cases. Erin shared a website (www.landmarkcases.org) and asked each of us to research two or more cases that our students might find relevant. We agreed to find cases that would satisfy several criteria. The cases had to be meaningful to our students' lives. Cases about topics foreign to our students' experiences would not provide the everyday life connections that we desired to make. In addition, the cases had to relate to the global concepts we had previously identified, including citizens' rights and responsibilities, effective communication, and the limitations of freedom. Finally, the connections between the cases we chose and the Bill of Rights had to be clear enough for seventh graders to find. Figure 6.2 explains our choices.

Once we had reached a consensus about the cases we'd examine, Erin reminded us about the importance of engaging students in the content.

"How are we going to keep this interesting for them?" she asked.

 After a few brainstorming sessions, we decided to use some carefully chosen theatrics and seemingly random events to build suspense.

Our unit began shortly after the December holiday break when Kathryn announced on the intercom: "We interrupt this regularly scheduled learning activity with a newsflash of great importance. Please tune in to W-P-I-G for a breaking story coming live to you from Topeka, Kansas. We have a feeling the events taking place are going to change history."

Our students were doubly intrigued when we flipped on the television sets connected to our computer presentation stations. They watched a video recording of one of Dutchtown's eighth graders impersonating Linda Brown of *Brown* fame. She described the long, desolate trek she took each day through a train yard to reach the school reserved for black students when there was a school reserved for white students located just minutes from her home. The injustices she endured became apparent as she spoke dramatically to our students.

Our seventh graders giggled at first because they recognized India, one of our former students, as a popular and perky cheerleader who never seemed to be upset about anything. By the time the video clip ended, their laughter had subsided and they were full of outrage and purpose. We gave each student a detective's notebook and asked them to jot down clues that would help them understand an important court case related to India's presentation. Though they didn't understand all that was happening, they played along because, as Samantha said, "It was something different."

Then we resumed our normal activities. Later that day, when our students had nearly forgotten about the initial interruption, a school staff member whom we had recruited buzzed each of our classrooms with a message from a "Mr. Brown." The exchange went something like this.

Featured Court Cases			
	Description of Case	**Citizenship Concept**	**Significance to Students (Rationale for Inclusion)**
Brown v. the Board of Education	Linda Brown was an African American student who wanted to attend an all-white school because it was closer to her home than the school designated for black students. The Topeka Board of Education denied her application because of her race. The Brown family believed this violated the rights guaranteed them by the Constitution, so they brought their complaints to court. Eventually, the Supreme Court decision of this case overturned the separate but equal precedent set by *Plessy v. Ferguson* in 1896. Segregation was no longer acceptable in public facilities such as schools.	Civil Rights	Our students are quite familiar with school policies, school board decisions, and race relations within our own school system. Many of their grandparents remember when schools in our district were segregated. This case is relevant to their lives because the setting and the issues of equality surrounding the case are concrete concepts they can understand.
New Jersey v. T.L.O	Two girls were found smoking in a school restroom, which was against school policy. The teacher took the girls to the principal's office where one of the girls admitted to smoking, but the other girl, T.L.O., refused to confess. The principal asked T.L.O. to open her purse. When she did, he saw a pack of cigarettes. When he removed the cigarettes from her purse, he noticed paraphernalia that he thought indicated involvement with marijuana. He then thoroughly searched T.L.O.'s purse. The girl admitted to selling drugs at school but claimed that the evidence collected from her purse during the search violated her Fourth Amendment rights. The court decision maintained that schools do not have to meet the same probable cause standard as police because schools are entrusted with protecting children.	Right to Privacy Search and Seizure	Our students believe that their right to privacy supercedes all other interests, even at school. They will often argue that they can keep anything in their backpacks because school personnel can't search their belongings without permission. This case introduced the legal terms *probable cause* and *search and seizure* and showed how these historically significant procedures relate to their own school experiences.
Texas v. Johnson	In 1984 Gregory Johnson was involved in a protest against the Reagan administration's policies. During the protest, Johnson doused an American Flag with kerosene and burned it. The protesting group shouted, "Red, white, and blue, we spit on you" as the flag burned. Witnesses were highly offended. Burning the flag was a violation of a Texas statute, and Johnson was convicted and sentenced to a year in jail and a $2,000 fine. The case was appealed to the Supreme Court, which ruled that burning the flag was a form of expression protected by the First Amendment of the Constitution.	Freedom of Expression	Our students are often confused by freedom of expression. They believe it means a person is able to say whatever he or she pleases. This case provided an opportunity to explore the responsibility that accompanies our rights. Our students were also able to explore the fact that tone is as important a part of communication as the statements we make with our words and actions.

Figure 6.2 Supreme Court Cases Studied as Part of Citizenship Focus

"Excuse me, Mrs. Edmonds?"

"Yes?"

"There is a Mr. Brown on the telephone. Says he's from Topeka, Kansas. He needs someone to complete some computations about distance and temperature that he can include in a letter he's preparing to send to the Topeka School Board office. I told him the Flying Pigs are working on converting measurements in math right now and might be able to help him."

"Sure, we'd love to help," Kathryn replied. "Please send the information to us."

Shortly thereafter, a student office worker showed up with a blank worksheet that our students then completed based on the detective clues and video observations (see Figure 6.3).

Afterward, we again continued with our regularly scheduled lessons. Later the same day, the school secretary entered our team area and dumped a stack of mail on our desks.

"Whew," she said, playing along, "this just arrived for the Flying Pigs. Would each of you please take one of these envelopes? I don't know what they are, but I was told that I had to deliver them to you immediately. They must be important."

Each envelope contained two letters. One was a handwritten appeal to the Topeka School Board by Linda Brown's mother. The other was a formal business letter written in response. These were not authentic primary source documents but those we had designed to provide additional information about the court case. Students recorded clues in their detective notebooks and, once again, we went right back to our regular work.

Each of these activities revealed key details about the landmark Supreme Court case. The information we planted was similar to what we would have shared in a lecture. But because we did not inundate them with facts or make the issues routine, we enabled students to record, process, and interpret the information throughout the day while having a bit of fun. The amusement and pacing of the activities also improved their retention.

All of our students experienced these events at the same time. We did not save the math clue for math class or the business letter for language arts. We made the events seem important and intriguing by allowing them to interrupt our regular class activities. We intentionally kept the students off balance because we wanted them to stay alert and interested. Otherwise, during the

Name_____ Date Feburary 13, 07 Group Orange

The following is a map of Linda Brown's house in Topeka, KS and the two different schools. Monroe Elementary was the school that Linda was forced to attend because it was the African American school regardless of how far away it was from her house. Sumner Elementary was only a few blocks away from her house, but African Americans were not allowed to attend. In order for the NAACP and Oliver Brown (Linda's father) to fight against this inequality, they need to find out the exact distance (in yards) from her home to each school, the time (in minutes) it takes Linda to walk to each school, and the severity of the cold weather conditions.

1. Linda had to walk 5,280 feet to Monroe Elementary, how many yards is this? 1760 yds.
2. If Linda was allowed to attend Sumner Elementary, which is only 7 blocks away, how many yards would she have to walk? (1 block= 60 feet) 140 yds
3. If it took Linda 1 minute and 30 seconds to walk 1 block, how long would it take Linda to walk 7 blocks? 10 min. 30 sec.
4. If it took Linda 1 minute and 30 seconds to walk 60 feet, how long would it take her to walk 5, 280 feet in minutes? 132 min
   in hours and minutes? 2 hr. 12 min
5. Linda had to walk through rain, snow, and really cold weather in order to attend Monroe Elementary. When Mr. Brown went to check the newspaper for the weather of one week in Topeka, KS, some of the data was missing. Fill in the missing temperatures in the chart below.

Weather for Topeka, KS

	Mon	Tue	Wed	Thu
36°F Overcast Wind: NE at 8 mph Humidity: 93%	38°F	3 °C	46 °F	8°C	19°F	-7 °C	52 °F	11°C

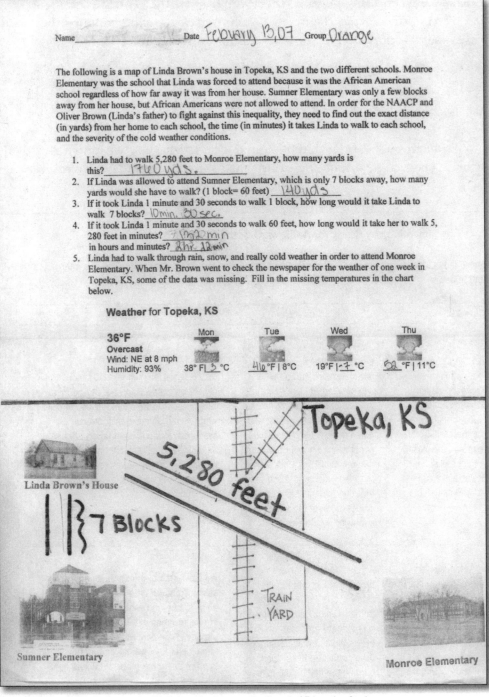

Linda Brown's House

7 Blocks

5,280 feet

Topeka, KS

TRAIN YARD

Sumner Elementary

Monroe Elementary

Figure 6.3 Measurement Conversion Worksheet for *Brown v. the Board of Education* Study

breaks between class periods, they would spoil the surprise for those who hadn't yet participated. Figure 6.4 summarizes the clues about other court cases that we provided to students during our classes.

Consider the context

Aside from the brief activities and dramatizations, we did not provide formal instruction about the court case on that first day. There were no

---

Introductory Clues for Additional Court Cases

Note: All clues held the element of surprise in that the clues were presented simultaneously within our classrooms and interrupted the natural flow of our lessons for the day.

Case	Clue #1	Clue #2	Clue #3
New Jersey v. T.L.O.	Kathryn entered our classrooms with two students who dramatized a scene in which students are caught smoking in the school restroom and are sent to the principal's office. This reenactment enabled the class to understand the case at hand because T.L.O. was accused of smoking and distributing drugs on campus.	Christine Wood, our team's paraprofessional, entered our classroom with a purse she claimed to have found outside on the playground. She told students, "There are notes in here. Let's see what conclusions we can draw about the contents." Students then read the notes and discovered that they were lists of fictional students whom T.L.O. had been supplying with drugs.	Mrs. Hughes, our school's 504 plan facilitator, called us on our cell phones, posing as T.L.O.'s mother. The phone calls were placed on the classroom speaker system so students could overhear her arguing that T.L.O.'s purse had been illegally searched without regard to search and seizure limitations protected by the Constitution.
Texas v. Johnson	Several of our students were enlisted to participate in a political demonstration in each of our classrooms. Students in the demonstration chanted slogans opposing the Reagan administration's policies during the 1980s. One student in the group carried an American flag.	A videotape of a news broadcast interrupted our classes, and the reporter (a former student) described the events that had occurred at the political demonstration in Texas, which ended in Johnson burning the flag on the steps of a government building.	We gave each of our students a bag of ashes (from our fireplaces) and allowed them to bury the ashes as onlookers of the flag burning in Texas had done on the day of the demonstration. During the burial ceremony, we played patriotic music to emphasize that many onlookers were offended by Johnson's actions.

Figure 6.4 Introductory Clues for Additional Court Cases

lectures, no pontifications on "Here's why it's important for you to hear this discussion." But just as we had hoped, our students were nevertheless buzzing with curiosity during recess and between classes.

"Hey, how many clues do you think we're going to get?"

"No telling."

"It's kinda weird that our teachers think we think this stuff is real, isn't it?"

"So, what's new?"

"At least it's not *real* work!"

The following day, our students spent time identifying and recording the perspectives represented by each side in *Brown*. Monique guided them.

"Now, if you were Linda Brown's family what would your argument be?" she asked. "What's their side of the story?"

Students offered suggestions, and Monique recorded their responses on the whiteboard. Students also updated their detective notebooks. After considering the issues from both perspectives, students reflected on the two opposing views. (See Figure 6.5 for a sample response.)

While she circulated around the classroom, Monique noticed that Regan had hesitated in writing her opinion. This was not typical behavior; Regan was usually one of the first to finish assignments. Monique asked if she needed help.

"Yes, I'm having trouble," Regan said thoughtfully. "I mean, do you want to know what I think now, or what I would have thought in 1954? Doesn't the time period change your perspective?"

Monique realized she couldn't have prompted this insight if she had tried. Other students quickly caught on.

"That's true," said Colby. "I think I would have a different opinion if I was a kid at the white school in 1954."

"I'll bet your opinion would have been different if you were one of the kids at the black school, too," Donovan interjected.

Suddenly our seventh graders, who rarely looked beyond their own interests, were collectively reflecting on the reasons people might hold opposing views. Not only were they beginning to understand the importance of perspective, they were using information from several subjects to reinforce this new knowledge. Here they were in language arts class exploring a landmark Supreme Court case from the history curriculum and identifying bias, a skill that was necessary for science. Our integration efforts were working!

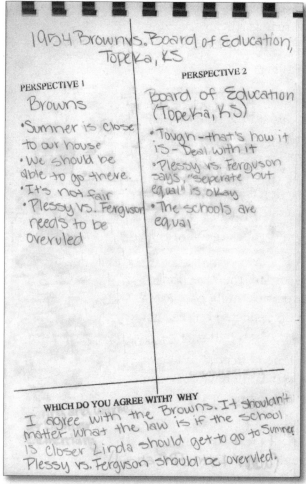

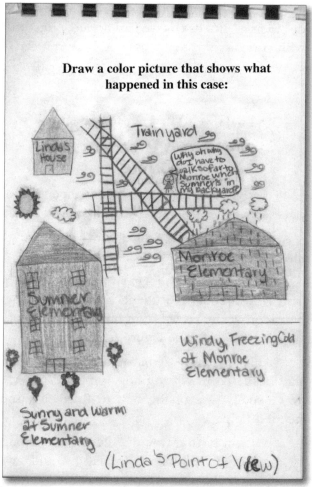

Figure 6.5 Worksheet for Comparing Perspectives in *Brown v. the Board of Education*

And we were only getting started. Next we shifted our focus to the Bill of Rights. Erin gave each student a copy of the amendments to analyze in relationship to the court case. Working in small groups, students created lists of the constitutional violations they found and explained their reasoning in writing. (See Figure 6.6 for a sample reflection.)

To end each Supreme Court case study that we reviewed during the unit, we asked nine students to wear black graduation robes and reenact the decisions. As the justices entered, we announced, "All rise as the honorable court enters the classroom." The justices took turns reading annotated versions of the official decisions.

Even being selected as a Supreme Court justice was a learning experience. Nominated students had to participate in simulated confirmation hearings before

Congress. Erin, acting as the president, chose the nominees based on class performance and participation. Each nominee had to report to the Senate chambers (our classrooms during our team planning period) and accurately answer questions about the role of the judiciary and the balance of power asserted in the Constitution. Eager to be included in this process, our students scrambled to learn the functions of the Supreme Court and eagerly participated in class discussions, hoping to receive a nomination.

Brown took place in 1954, a time when all Supreme Court justices were white males. To remain true to history, our nominees and appointments reflected the court's composition. During the confirmation process, none of our students noticed the lack of diversity. When the justices entered the classrooms to deliver a verdict, however, Brandon blurted out, "Hey, why are there only white boys up there? That doesn't seem fair."

Michelle quickly answered, "Don't you get it? This was 1954. That's how it actually was. There were no black justices on the Supreme Court. There weren't any women either!"

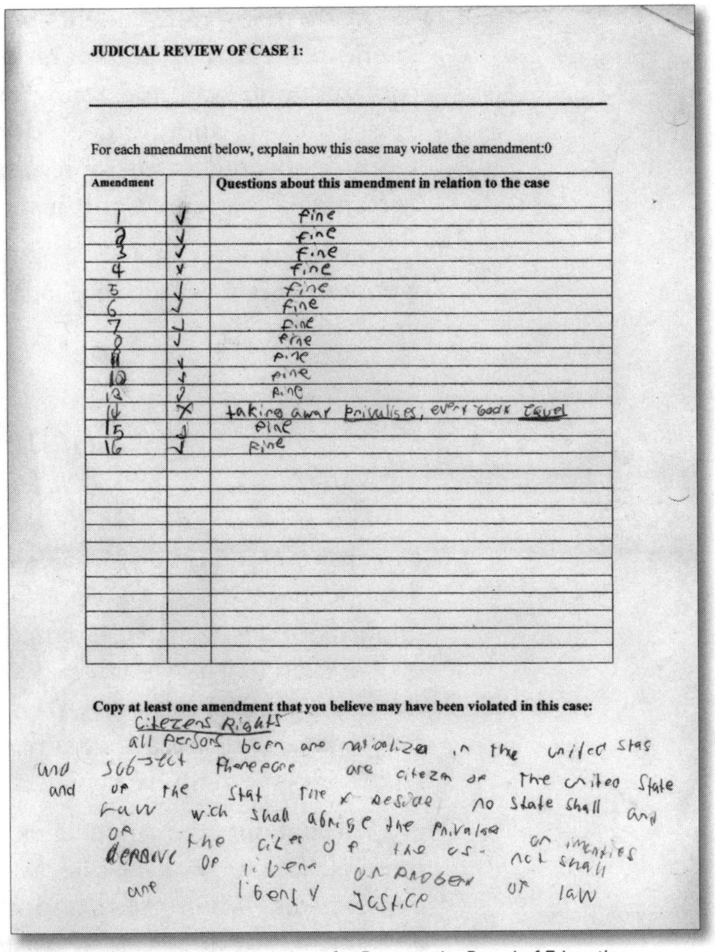

JUDICIAL REVIEW OF CASE 1:

For each amendment below, explain how this case may violate the amendment:0

Amendment		Questions about this amendment in relation to the case
1	✓	fine
2	✓	fine
3	✓	fine
4	✓	fine
5	✓	fine
6	✓	fine
7	✓	fine
8	✓	fine
11	✓	fine
10	✓	fine
13	✓	fine
14	X	taking away privalises, every body equel
15	✓	fine
16	✓	fine

Copy at least one amendment that you believe may have been violated in this case:

Citezens Rights

all persons born and nationalized in the united stas and subject therefore are citezen of the united state and of the stat thre resside no state shall and faw wich shall abrige the privalege or imenities of the citez of the US. not shall deprive or liberty or proberty or law and liberty justice

Figure 6.6 Judicial Review Worksheet for *Brown v. the Board of Education*

"Hey, yeah," said Matt, "but this case started to change that, didn't it?"

Michelle and Matt had made two very important observations, which proved they had internalized the case's impact. They understood that opportunities for minorities were limited in the 1950s, and they also realized that it was due to cases like *Brown v. the Board of Education* that opportunities expanded for minority citizens. The changes were reflected in our following court case, *New Jersey v. T.L.O.*, which took place in 1984. During this case study, our two eldest justices were forced into retirement and were replaced with the first black justice and the first female justice. Our students noted the number of years that had passed between *Brown v. the Board of Education* and *New Jersey v. T.L.O.* and realized that change is slow.

At the time, our students were studying proportion in math, and Kacie interjected that this configuration of justices, though fairer than the 1950s configuration, was not a proportional representation of American society. This led to yet another deep discussion when Darrien, bringing up another recently covered math topic, asked, "What is the probability of a woman becoming a Supreme Court justice?"

As a team, we got busy answering that question. And nobody had to wonder whether we were addressing standards through our curriculum integration.

Connecting the Dots

Though we had carefully mapped the curriculum so we could blend the citizenship standard into our lessons during the third grading period, we were astounded by the many opportunities we found along the way to connect important concepts. The original ideas from our team meeting continued to evolve each day as we interacted with students. We were not all working on the collaborative unit every day, every hour, to the same degree. Some days, only one teacher would actually refer to the main topics and then only briefly. Other days, we'd all be involved.

Throughout the nine-week grading period, we remained alert for interdisciplinary links while addressing specific standards and curriculum benchmarks. When these opportunities arose, we seized the moments. As a result, we were able to consistently relate our daily lessons to our global concept so that our students developed a deep understanding of the standards. Figure 6.7 shows how we fit the pieces together.

Figure 6.7 provides just a sampling of the activities students completed as part of our citizenship focus. Though we included many possibilities on the curriculum map, we didn't plan all the lessons that eventually became part of our unit. As our collaborative instruction evolved, we followed tangents that we hadn't considered in our planning. Later, we added these developments to our curriculum map so we would have a record of the changes. We had to continually remind ourselves that it was okay to stray from our original plans to take advantage of teachable moments.

Interdisciplinary Links to the Citizenship Focus

Citizenship Integrated Unit—Supreme Court Cases

Guiding Standard from History Curriculum:

Students develop an understanding of the structure and purposes of government, the foundations of the American democratic system, and the role of the United States in the world while learning about the rights and responsibilities of citizenship.

Related Standards

History	Science	Math	Language Arts
H-1.Students develop a spatial understanding of Earth's surface and the processes that shape it, the connections between people and places, and the relationship between man and his environment. H-2.Students develop a sense of historical perspective as they study the history of their community, state, nation, and world.	S-1.The students will become aware of the characteristics and life cycles of organisms and understand their relationships to each other and to their environment. S-2.In learning environmental science, students will develop an appreciation of the natural environment and learn the importance of environmental quality, and acquire a sense of stewardship. As consumers and citizens, they will be able to recognize how our personal, professional, and political actions affect the natural world.	M-1.In problem-solving investigations, students demonstrate an understanding of the concepts, processes, and real-life applications of measurement. M-2.In problem-solving investigations, students demonstrate an understanding of geometric concepts and applications involving one-, two-, and three-dimensional geometry, and justify their findings. M-3.In problem-solving investigations, students discover trends, formulate conjectures regarding cause-and-effect relationships, and demonstrate critical thinking skills in order to make informed decisions. M-4.In problem-solving investigations, students demonstrate an understanding of patterns, relations, and functions that represent and explain real-world situations.	LA-1.Students read, comprehend, and respond to a range of materials using a variety of strategies for different purposes. LA-2.Students write competently for a variety of purposes and audiences. LA-3.Students locate, select, and synthesize information from a variety of texts, media, references, and technological sources to acquire and communicate knowledge. LA-4.Students read, analyze, and respond to literature as a record of life experiences. LA-5.Students apply reasoning and problem-solving skills to reading, writing, speaking, listening, viewing, and visually representing.

(Louisiana Administrative Code 2005)

Figure 6.7 Interdisciplinary Links to the Citizenship Focus, Part 1

A Sampling of Class Activities Integrating Core Classes to Global Concept of Citizenship	
Related Lessons	**Related Standards**
History 1. Introduction of three landmark Supreme Court cases (*Brown v. the Board of Education*, *New Jersey v. T.L.O.*, *Texas v. Johnson*) in all core classes. Clues for each case were introduced through preplanned activities that interrupted our regularly scheduled lessons. Students recorded information on specially designed notepads so they would have complete information about each case by the end of the introductory activities.	H-2, H-3, LA-1, LA-2, LA-4, LA-5
2. For each case, students completed mini–judicial reviews. Students received a copy of the constitutional amendments so they could search for any violation of rights indicated in the presented cases.	H-2, H-3, LA-3, LA-5
3. After reviewing *Brown v. the Board of Education*, students were given several open-ended scenarios involving equal opportunity for people of different genders, handicaps, and races. Students wrote essays to describe the events that should occur to ensure that all parties involved in the scenarios received equal opportunities.	H-2, H-3, LA-1, LA-2, LA-5
4. As part of our study of *New Jersey v. T.L.O.*, a DEA agent visited our team to discuss search and seizure procedures, guidelines for undercover operations, and rights of the citizen, the accused, and the government.	H-3, LA-4
Math 1. During the clue introduction for *Brown v. the Board of Education*, students were required to complete measurement conversions involving temperatures, distances, and time. (See Figure 6.3.)	H-1, H-2, H-3, M-1, M-4
2. During our study of *New Jersey v. T.L.O.*, students researched cancer rates related to smoking. They took the information they had gathered and reported the data in various mathematical formats, converting the data from decimals to fractions and percentages.	H-3, M-3, M-4, S-1, LA-1, LA-3,
3. Using graphs that showed cancer rates among different population subgroups, students calculated the number of teenaged smokers represented in the data. Then they assumed the role of responsible citizens as they wrote persuasive letters to teenagers, urging them not to smoke and using the data gathered from their research to support their antismoking stance.	H-3, S-1, M-3, M-4, LA-2, LA-3,
4. During our study of *Texas v. Johnson*, students used the concepts of scale and proportion to create flag drawings of various sizes. They completed their scale drawings in chalk around the school campus and added citizenship-related slogans to their creations.	M-1, M-2

Figure 6.7 Interdisciplinary Links to the Citizenship Focus, Part 2

Language Arts	1. Students read the novel *Witness*, which provided historical perspective about race relations in the early 1900s. In addition, the novel enabled students to explore and define the concept of equality as it pertains to the Constitution, Declaration of Independence, and the Bill of Rights. Students were asked to identify the perspectives of various characters and justify those perspectives based on the characters' experiences, thus providing them with a necessary science skill.	H-2, H-3, LA-1, LA-2, LA-3, LA-4, LA-5
	2. Students read "The Lady or the Tiger" and compared the judicial system described in the short story to the American judicial system that would be used in *Witness* if one of the characters had been on trial for crimes committed.	H-2, H-3, LA-1, LA-2, LA-3, LA-5
	3. Students created circle graphs depicting their opinions of the trial outcome in "The Lady or the Tiger." In the graphs, they indicated whether the man on trial had encountered a lady and should be declared innocent or whether he had encountered a tiger and should be found guilty. Creating the graphs first involved a discussion of the probability of the king's system and changes in probability that might occur based on characters' manipulations (namely the princess) of trial events. Students tallied the data in class, converted the information to percentages, and created circle graphs to display their results.	H-3, M-3, M-4, LA-3, LA-5
	4. Prior to the introduction of *Texas v. Johnson*, while studying symbolism in language arts, students read historical information about the American flag and guidelines for its proper care and disposal. In addition, students followed written directions for creating five-point stars with a single scissor cut. Students placed facts about the American flag on the stars and placed them around the classroom. Afterward, students discussed why the flag was an important symbol and what the flag represented for American citizens.	H-2, H-3, LA-1, LA-3
Science	1. A state wildlife and fisheries agent visited our team and explained the connections between wildlife data sampling completed by scientists and laws written by legislators. He also explained how the laws, in turn, protect animal populations. In addition, he discussed with students citizens' rights and responsibilities in relation to the environment.	H-1, H-3, S-1, S-2, M-3, LA-5
	2. Using problem-solving skills, students brainstormed various methods of controlling Colorado's elk population, such as making decisions based on sampling data to decide whether or not predators should be reintroduced and adjusting hunting limits. Students were required to consider their responsibilities as citizens as part of their solutions to the overpopulation of elk herds.	H-1, S-1, S-2, M-3, LA-3, LA-5
	3. Students considered the various fictional and nonfictional characters' perspectives as part of their discussions about whether humans have acted responsibly in protecting the environment. First they read *Brother Eagle, Sister Sky* and discussed Chief Seattle's actions to preserve the environment in the absence of formal laws. They compared Chief Seattle's beliefs to current environmental regulations. Then students were asked if Chief Seattle would have approved of the king in "The Lady or the Tiger" introducing an exotic species into his environment for judicial purposes. Students also wrote essays in response to the following prompts: *In "The Lady or the Tiger," suppose the king brought in an exotic animal as part of his judicial system. Explain how this animal could affect the native animals that live in the kingdom.* *Word gets back to Chief Seattle about the introduction of exotic species by the king, and Chief Seattle is angry. Why do you think he is so upset? Be specific and justify your reasoning with specific examples.* *If Chief Seattle were to put the king on trial for this crime against nature, what kind of judicial system do you think he would use? Design it.*	H-1, H-2, H-3, S-1, S-2, LA-1, LA-2, LA-3, LA-4, LA-5

Figure 6.7 Part 2 (continued)

Sometimes opportunities arose from students' observations and inquiries. One day, for example, Jean Paul blurted out in class, "Oh my gosh! I just realized it. I can't believe it!"

"What?" several students asked him.

"I've been looking at that letter all year long because I face that same bulletin board every day. I just realized that those books donated to St. Bernard Parish came from Topeka, Kansas! That's weird, isn't it?"

Indeed, through our Love of Literacy campaign, we had received many donated books to distribute to libraries destroyed by Hurricane Katrina. A photograph and letter from one contributing school hung on the board directly across from Jean Paul's desk.

"No, that's not *weird*," said Blaze. "Isn't it irony?"

This led to a wonderful student-generated discussion about whether irony was an appropriate term to describe the coincidence. These types of spontaneous teachable moments occurred more and more frequently as we explored the citizenship standard.

Other times we were the ones who would burst into team meetings gushing about some wonderful connection to the standard that we had just experienced in class. This was the case on the day our students dissected owl pellets in science to collect data about mouse populations. Erin suddenly realized that laws are based on the data scientists collect as they attempt to control animal populations. Although she had mentioned this in class, she knew she should validate this connection for students, so she invited a wildlife and fisheries officer to visit. As Erin requested, he explained how hunting limits are directly related to the work of scientists and lawmakers. However, unexpectedly, the officer provided background knowledge for our next Supreme Court case, *New Jersey v. T.L.O.* While explaining the importance of having hunting limits, the officer mentioned that it was within his legal responsibility to search hunters and fishermen and their vehicles to ensure that they were respecting the limits.

"Hey, don't you have to have a search warrant to check someone's boat?" Robert asked him. "Isn't that like their house?"

Dylan, who hunts frequently, answered for him. "A wildlife and fisheries officer can look in all of your stuff if you're hunting or fishing," he said. "It doesn't matter what you say."

The agent explained how government tried to balance search and seizure laws with the need to maintain animal populations. Here was another connection between our citizenship unit and science that we had not anticipated but were thrilled that our students could discover.

Throughout the unit, we modeled our thought processes when exploring the relationships among connected topics. Eventually, students exercised their brains on their own initiative.

One spontaneous leap occurred as students read "The Lady or the Tiger" and tried to make sense of the medieval king's imposition of a twisted justice system. In the story, the accused must choose between two doors, one concealing a lady, the other concealing a tiger. Choosing the tiger results in a guilty verdict.

While we were reading the story aloud in class one day, Colby called out, "Hey! That's a violation of at least two amendments in the Bill of Rights!"

"Which ones?" Monique asked him.

"Well, one is the right to a fair trial and the other one is about cruel and unusual punishment," he said without hesitation. "I mean, being eaten by a tiger? Please!"

Joey chimed in, "But, Colby, think of perspective. In ancient times that was not cruel or unusual. You're thinking like it's 2007, not 1500."

In a single moment, Colby and Joey had connected all the major focal points for this unit: the Bill of Rights, perspective, and the evaluation of judicial systems. Monique had planned for students to compare the judicial system in the story to the U.S. court system and evaluate violations of the Bill of Rights in a formal assignment. Colby and Joey had beaten her to the punch. Figure 6.8 reflects the activities that students completed next.

Admittedly, an assignment requiring so much evaluation and higher-level thinking might seem quite daunting for special needs students. However, our students had been applying these concepts in every core class. Because the information was on their minds throughout the school day, they did not flinch at the assignment. On the contrary, all of our students made curricular connections that we had not anticipated.

Our students realized that every teacher on the team knew what was happening in all the other classrooms, so they willingly brought up the connections, trusting that we'd know what they were talking about. The same week we read "The Lady or the Tiger" in language arts, students were wrestling with probability in math. In the midst of the math lesson, Foster exasperatedly asked Kathryn, "So this man's life is left up to probability? You mean to tell me he has only a fifty-fifty chance of living? So what makes this king's court a fair trial? They might as well have flipped a coin!"

Cumulative Discussion Guide—"The Lady or the Tiger" and Branches of Government

In your groups, complete the following activities to prepare for our share circle.

1. Complete a Venn diagram to compare the **judicial** systems of "The Lady or the Tiger" and *Witness*. Then proceed to number 2.

2. Use the **Bill of Rights** to complete the following chart.

	Amendments Violated	Proof
***Witness*, p. 59**		
"The Lady or the Tiger"		

3. Which of the branches of government is the king's role in "The Lady or the Tiger" most like? (executive, legislative, judicial)

   Give a specific event from the story that provides proof that he serves this role.

4. Read the article about habeas corpus (in your history books, p. 233). Then, answer the question that follows.

Figure 6.8 Cumulative Discussion Guide

The Supreme Court has clearly established that trials must be free from a coercive or intimidating atmosphere. It also has ruled that disruptive activity at trial by the press can render a trial unfair.

What argument for habeas corpus could be used by the accused people in *Witness* and in "The Lady or the Tiger"?

Story	Reason to believe the person had an unfair trial	Is the system of that society likely to support a habeas corpus claim? Why?
Witness		
"The Lady or the Tiger"		

5. Evidence is important in all trials. We know that the princess's lover was guilty of the crime with which he was charged. Now it's time to use evidence to decide whether the man was found guilty or innocent.

Use **the princess's perspective** to provide evidence from the story to support each outcome.

Guilty—Tiger	Innocent—Lady
1.	1.
2.	2.
3.	3.

So, did the young man choose the lady or the tiger? _____

Figure 6.8 continued

Foster didn't stop to wonder whether Kathryn would know what was happening in language arts or that Monique would understand a question about probability. Everything was related. When wrapping up the class discussion of the short story, students created circle graphs indicating whether they believed the accused young man met the lady or the tiger when he opened the door of fate. This short assessment reviewed skills that had been addressed earlier in the year, namely percentages and graphing. After examining the graphs, Foster thoughtfully underscored the impact of what he had learned.

"Well, look at that," he said and sighed. "Of all three classes, the greatest probability of living that we gave this poor dude was the same fifty-fifty chance that the original author did. We didn't improve his chance of living at all."

Foster's comments captured our own feelings about traditional methods of integrating the curriculum. Had we unintentionally given our students only a fifty-fifty chance of achieving deep understanding because of the limitations of our previous unit designs? Were we so intent on presenting pretty interdisciplinary packages that we forgot to reinforce the messages inside?

Perhaps our students had always been capable of making deep connections among the concepts they were learning, but we had not provided them with the right focus. The same standards movement we originally rebelled against had helped us improve our practices and provide a stronger foundation for student achievement. In the process, we discovered that effective interdisciplinary teaching is more messy than neat. It doesn't need to be prepackaged and adorned in order for students to make connections.

ChapterSeven
"Everything Is Related"

In October 2006, we attended a week-long professional development institute sponsored by the Disney Corporation. We were nervous about leaving our students for so long and consequently left behind hefty assignments so they would not have time to misbehave.

When we returned to school the following week, we were surprised by our students' reactions.

"You gave us busy work," they complained. "We never do busy work in here. We always do real stuff."

"We can do the hard stuff, you know, even if you aren't here."

"Please let us do real work next time. Don't you trust us?"

Ouch. That was not the message we had intended to send. Instead of giving our students a chance to demonstrate their increasing maturity and respect for our team values, we had let fearful teacher logic sneak into our planning. We had assumed that without our physical presence acting as a deterrent our students—or at least a few difficult characters—would give the substitute teachers a hard time.

As we reflected, we realized how similar our views were to those expressed by colleagues over the years. Often, when other teachers consider our approach to curriculum integration, they cite fear of student misbehavior as one of the biggest obstacles to overcome.

"My students won't be able to do this because they are too disruptive," some have said.

"I'd love to do all those cool activities with my students, but Johnny won't be able to handle it," others have mentioned. "He'll get everyone all riled up."

We can understand their reluctance to change. Let's face it: misbehavior in the middle grades is like a cold germ just waiting for a chance to infect healthy cells. It hovers around classrooms and looks for an opening. A few determined troublemakers can spoil a good lesson plan before the ink dries on your planner. And who are the students with the best attendance rates? Class clowns and miscreants tend to dominate the list. They rarely seem to miss a day of school, which means our peaceful kingdom can come under attack at any moment. Trying to predict whether their antics will throw off the team's equilibrium can prompt premature panic and cause teachers to retreat to familiar terrain.

Sometimes keeping disruptive students confined to their desks seems the only solution to averting chaos. Limiting these students' freedom prevents the contagion from spreading, or so we tell ourselves. But a closer examination of the causes of misbehavior suggests another approach.

We have discovered that the students with the greatest discipline problems tend to be bright adolescents who get bored waiting for their peers to learn. Other major troublemakers have fallen behind in a particular subject or in multiple classes and disrupt our activities to deflect attention from their inadequacies. In other words, it's what they know or don't know about the content that typically causes adolescents to act out. And this is a symptom that good interdisciplinary teaching can cure.

Addressing the extremes in our school populations can be quite challenging, but in our experience, engaged students usually are well-behaved students. Team-based, collaborative planning is the best method we have found for providing developmentally appropriate instruction for all students. Discipline becomes self-generated rather than teacher imposed.

Thoughtful curriculum integration enables students to understand our lessons' relevance and actively search for connections between subjects. Because they are busy exercising their minds, they are much less distracted than when the instruction demands their rote responses. The impact of this different approach is demonstrated through the changing behavior of advanced students, such as Porter. Instead of resorting to his habit of acting out because he was bored, Porter began suggesting deeper questions for the class to explore.

"Hey, you know how in *Flowers for Algernon* they made Charlie smarter?" he called out one day. "I wonder if they can really do that now with genetic engineering. That's what we're studying in Mrs. Babin's class. Do y'all think we should ask her?"

Interdisciplinary teaching also provides a stronger structure to support our special needs students. Rather than being confused by their peers' attempts to engage in abstract reasoning, they learn how to contribute to intellectual conversations without fear of ridicule. Continual collaboration gives them greater confidence to try. Instead of a traditional classroom culture where a few students dominate discussions and seem to know all the answers, effective teams encourage everyone to wonder.

"Would you want intelligence to be increased in real life?" Andrew, a quiet, special needs student responded to Porter's inquiry. "I mean, Charlie was still a freak to everyone once he was smart. Is it better to be really smart than sort of dumb? I'm not sure if genetic engineering could do this anyway. Didn't Charlie have an operation in the story? That's not genetic engineering, is it?"

In the old days, such sophisticated thinking from students with identified learning disabilities would have astonished us. Now it fuels our team's growth and proves that young adolescents are far more capable than most adults assume. Many students have gaps in their knowledge and skills, and we still provide remediation on our team. But that's not *all* we do. We don't dumb down the curriculum for struggling students. We use integration to help them progress.

A Curriculum Wake-Up Call

By the second nine-week grading period, our students typically understand that we might address any subject in any classroom. It is not taboo to mention math in history or science in language arts. So when a student asks in language arts class about the probability of a certain character's reaction or asks in science class how Chief Seattle might have reacted to the environmental issues discussed in the readings, we are ready to assist them in discovering the answers. With the supports provided by instructional teams, all students are capable of making deep connections to the content and experiencing academic success.

Consider the growth experienced by Earl, a special needs student who was so concerned about maintaining his cool reputation among his peers that he had been reluctant to let them think he might actually learn something in school. Consistent exposure to curriculum integration finally broke through his reserve.

In Monique's language arts class, students had been discussing symbolism. To make the concept more concrete, she introduced several American symbols and discussed the emotional connections people have to them. Then she referred to emotional symbols in literature. The chosen symbol for the day was the American flag. Students read about the flag's history, followed written directions to create a five-pointed star with paper, and wrote facts about the recommended care of the flag on each of the stars.

As Monique was hanging the stars on the bulletin board, Earl looked up sleepily from his desk and said, "Hey . . . I know why we're doing this. We're about to have a court case about the American flag, aren't we?"

Monique was taken aback.

"What on earth are you talking about, Earl?" she asked, feigning ignorance of the integrated unit (explained in Chapter 6) that our team had planned to explore through several landmark U.S. Supreme Court cases.

"Well, Mrs. Babin just gave us our court-case notebooks back this morning, and suddenly we're talking about flags in here. I know we've been talking about symbols and all, but I think our next court case will be about the flag."

Monique smiled at Earl and marveled at his prescient observation. How had he figured out our strategy in his semiconscious daze? We had indeed planned to introduce an important court case the following morning. In *Texas v. Johnson*, the court considered the implications of the American flag burning to protest the Republican National Convention in 1984. Trying to keep a few surprises up our sleeves, we had not mentioned this to students. We had been busy setting the scene. But Earl had quite unexpectedly, quite marvelously jumped ahead.

"Shhhh . . . Don't tell anyone," Monique whispered as she pulled Earl off to the side.

Earl winked and smiled slyly, "Nah, who'd believe me anyway?"

We rewarded Earl's astuteness by giving him a lead role in the protest march reenacted in our classrooms the following morning. At one point, Earl bellowed, "I'm here in Dallas, Texas, to protest the Reagan policies . . . or something like that!" The class laughed, but they all remembered why people were protesting in 1984.

The curricular connections that our students make are rarely random. Rather, they result from the system of supports that we have put in place through interdisciplinary teaming. By working together, we can prop up the students who are wobbly, keep others moving steadily on course, and remove the training wheels for those who are ready to race ahead. Shifting gears constantly and consciously is difficult in any classroom arrangement, but navigation gets easier when you have help from colleagues. On our team, including Kathryn as a full-time special education teacher provides an extra boost.

Visitors to our team are often surprised when they discover that about one-third of our students have identified learning disabilities. Most of our students also are unaware of these labels. Partly that's because Kathryn guides all students, not just those in the special education population. She doesn't draw attention to a selected group, and we don't alter our expectations that all students can produce high-quality work.

Every student participates in group activities and class discussions. Our special education students are never isolated from the general population. Kathryn both coteaches lessons and monitors students individually. She looks at instruction through the lens of confusion: What could be tripping up one or more students? Once she identifies a problem, she focuses on strategies such as visualization, summarization, or graphic organizers that can get students back on track.

Kathryn doesn't limit her outreach to students who qualify for special assistance, nor do we refer to her as a special education teacher. This would make it obvious to everyone that we consider some students deficient, and Kathryn's assistance would carry a stigma. Instead we call her our learning styles specialist. It might seem like a game of semantics, but it works. Students who are struggling for one reason or another don't hesitate to approach Kathryn for help. The groups she pulls aside for reinforcement include students with a wide range of ability levels. The groups are fluid and dynamic; membership is determined by need, not by a particular program designation. As previously mentioned, careful attention to students' academic needs also improves their behavior.

Every Student Can Soar

David's story beautifully illustrates this process. When David entered seventh grade, his academic future looked bleak. He struggled with basic skills in all subjects. We requested testing for special education services, but ultimately he did not qualify.

In the meantime, we subjected him to the full onslaught of our "You can do it" campaign by writing notes; saying, "You are so smart"; and using his best work as examples. We pulled him aside for extra help when we noticed his confusion or when he specifically requested assistance. David's performance began to improve, and we withdrew our request for special education testing.

Throughout the school year, David participated in our Academic Success Plan, which required students to help each other while working in pairs or small groups. David still asked for help, but increasingly he also assisted other students with math problems or reading guides.

The spring testing period came and went. In Louisiana the high-stakes exam determines whether a student can pass to the next grade level. David was visibly nervous when the scores or the consequences were mentioned.

In May we were ecstatic to learn that all of our students had passed the exam, including every special education student. Triumphant, we marched into our classrooms and shouted, "What is our team motto?"

They replied, "No Martian will fail!"

"That's right," we told them. "No one did."

Our students were stunned into silence. Then they began jumping and screaming as we passed out the proof. David stared at his score sheet and wept.

"Look at this," he said and hugged us each in turn. "Thank you, thank you."

Not only had he passed the test, he had scored in the eightieth percentile in both math and language arts.

David advanced to high school, and as a senior he served as president of the student government. He also went to college.

Integrated instructional teams give us the means to succeed with the other Davids in our schools, those students who will fall through the cracks without an array of intentional supports from conscientious and collaborative teachers. Filling in the gaps requires that we focus on our students as individuals and continually reflect on the global concepts that will help each of our students become productive citizens. Teaming helps us maintain our focus and assist our students in realizing that the concepts we study in class now will benefit them when they become adults. Unless we make the connections for our students in every class, they will not see how the themes they are studying relate to one another, and they will not grasp the abstract ideas that unify these topics. When our students begin to see the connections for themselves, we are satisfied that our teamwork has truly benefited them.

After we discussed *Texas v. Johnson* in class, Kathryn asked students why they thought so many people were upset that Johnson burned the American flag. Nicholas piped up, "Because, like, dude, it was, like, THE AMERICAN FLAG! Like, you can't hurt something people have so much emotion about."

An odd expression took over Nicholas's face as though he'd just made an extremely important realization. Then he blurted, "And, like, oh, it's symbolism like we were talking about yesterday! And, like, emotions matter, and . . . " Now he jumped to his feet. "Everything is related to something on this team!"

Yes! Everything is related because we are a true collaborative team. Working together helps make learning interesting, engaging, and relevant. Insights such as Nicholas's brilliant revelation confirm that our methods are working. These are the moments we wait for. Nothing inspires students and teachers more than success.

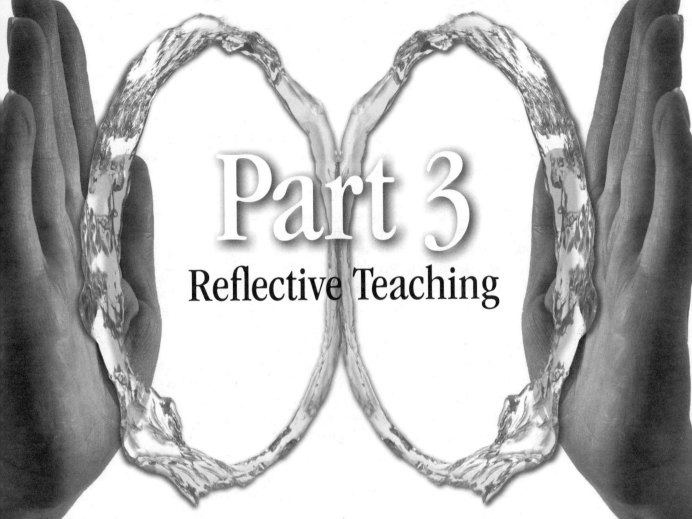

Part 3
Reflective Teaching

As humans, our natural desire is to reach toward the top, to explore the next frontier. While this drive undoubtedly leads to some of society's greatest innovations, it also can cause us to ignore the challenges directly in front of us. As a teaching team, we have discovered that the greatest riches in education often lie within the depth and unity of our professional practices rather than in the height of our individual achievements. We still seek to soar, but we recognize that growth withers without a solid root system.

Building strong relationships and connecting the content represent the first two sides of the teamwork triangle. The third part of the equilateral framework is reflective teaching. We consider reflection a form of job-embedded professional development. It is the tool that enables us to dig deeper, to figure out where we are individually and collectively.

Rarely will a team function well in all areas simultaneously. For example, the same year that we achieved a deep level of relationship building with students and their families through the use of surveys, Portfolio Show-Off Day, and student-led conferences, we reached only a superficial level of curriculum integration, such as naming the characters in math word problems after those in our language arts novel. Reflection helped us identify and close the gaps.

Effective teachers always ask themselves why they are doing what they are doing through questions that go beyond immediate utility ("Does it work?") to consider the ways in which instruction is working, why it is working, and for whom it is working (Zeichner and Liston 1996). This "Where do we go from here?" mind-set keeps our team in a reflective mode and motivates us to continually plunge beneath the surface.

Of course it's easier to reflect on the previous year and make plans for the future when team members stay put. Consistency creates comfort and a unified starting point for the new school year. But what happens when—cue the scary music—a team member leaves and an "unknown" joins the crew; or worse, a team splits up entirely?

First, understand that such changes are bound to happen. Life choices, changes in school leadership, and shifting student populations can always lead to turnover. Second, accept the fact that the depth of your team practices will vary as members come and go. Each time you will need to adjust, redefine your norms, and set goals that you jointly and consistently carry out. Finally, realize that if a team has been successful, its members may be asked to "spread the wealth." This might involve serving as a model team for the school and leading professional development sessions for colleagues. It also might lead to new tasks and challenges.

The success we have shared as a team has opened new opportunities for all of us. In the fall of 2007 Monique began coordinating the staff development for the same school in which Amanda had been appointed as associate principal. Kathryn stayed at Dutchtown Middle School and joined an eighth-grade team that planned to incorporate full inclusion of special education students for the first time.

Colleagues have asked us how we will be able to cope without each other. The answer is we won't be alone even though we may be apart. We will continue to share our achievements and struggles, just as we always have. Professional reflection is the thread that ties us together. This unbreakable bond gives us the courage to keep asking, "So, where do we go from here?"

ChapterEight
Looking in the Mirror

As educators, we do not dictate all the circumstances of our professional lives. We can't control our students' family backgrounds. We can't mandate the curricula. We can't always choose our room assignments or our schedules. The only thing we can truly control is the quality of our teaching.

Yet, many times we are afraid to bring up the issue of teachers' effectiveness in our discussions about school improvement because a small voice inside us suggests that other factors have a greater impact on students' success. In reality, however, teacher quality is the most critical component of all and, truly, is the only one we can change. Recent research has made a compelling case for focusing on the quality of instruction in our schools. Three years of effective teaching can improve student achievement rates by 35 to 50 percent (Sanders and Horn 1994). Robert Marzano (2003) highlighted multiple studies comparing the results different teachers achieved when working with students from similar socioeconomic backgrounds. Research shows that the most effective teachers guided their students to 72 percent pass rates while ineffective teachers got just 27 percent of their students to proficiency levels. Clearly, quality teaching can make a significant difference in school improvement and student achievement.

Unfortunately, we have become so focused on ensuring that all students have "highly qualified" teachers that we've forgotten the importance of ensuring that they also have highly effective teachers. Teacher quality is not just about the degrees or certifications a person has earned. Of greater importance is the impact teachers have on students' learning. As educators, we must be willing to look deeply at our practices and be brave enough to ask: Did every student in my class advance at least one grade level this year? How do I know? What evidence can I provide of my effectiveness as a teacher?

Instead of using such inquiries to improve our practices, many of us continue searching for scapegoats. At a recent national conference where the participants were discussing what to do about low-performing schools, a teacher suggested that districts should simply shift more high-achieving students into the schools' attendance zones.

"But that does not fix the problem," Amanda said. "The other kids are still not achieving."

"Can we change that?" the teacher asked.

Amanda's response was shocked and automatic: "If teachers do not make a difference, if we cannot improve student achievement, why are we here?"

That question goes to the core of our beliefs about teamwork. If we allow despair to overcome our purpose, we might as well pack away our lesson planners and go into another line of work. Yet in saying that, we do not mean to dismiss the frequent frustrations of teaching. No one succeeds every day with every student. And those of us who serve an abundance of struggling students have to work extra hard to beat back the blues when our best plans break down. Then we have to figure out why we missed the mark.

Analysis is essential for effective teaching. But isolated reflection isn't enough. We need help from colleagues, educators who are committed to excellence and professional reflection. Critiquing one another's practices can be frightening at first, but through teamwork you can develop the trust and refine the techniques that lead to improvement.

One of the most intense examples of this type of professional growth is the certification process for the National Board for Professional Teaching Standards (www.nbpts.org), which Monique and Amanda completed in 1999 and 2002 respectively. The process includes submission of an instructional portfolio in the chosen content area. The portfolio consists of four sections. Two of the sections require the teacher to videotape lessons and analyze the content for evidence of impact on student achievement. A third section seeks evidence of how well students learned throughout a unit. The final section focuses on the teacher as a learner, as a member of a professional community, and as a partner in working with parents. The portfolio usually takes about six months to complete. Afterward, the teacher also must pass an examination.

The entire National Board process is thorough and rigorous, but nothing compares to the experience of filming and viewing your instruction in action. Trust us, watching a videotape of your actual classroom practices will strip away any illusions of perfection that you may have as a teacher. Our National Board certification efforts revealed flaws that we would have rather swept under the rug. Yet the insights we gained during this period of deep professional reflection continue to shape our successes today. Years after achieving National Board certification, we still recall those monumental moments of clarity that challenged and changed us. One example occurred during the fall of our first year working together as a team.

A teacher's tears can be a discomfiting sight for students, and our students knew something was wrong when they walked into Amanda's second-period math class one day and saw her flushed face and bloodshot eyes. They exchanged knowing looks as they glanced at the video camera perched on a tripod in a corner of the classroom. They were well aware of the anxiety-producing inanimate observer that had become a permanent fixture on the team while Amanda completed the National Board certification requirements.

"So, Mrs. Mayeaux, you okay?" one of the boys ventured.

"Yes, but the lesson really flopped last period, and I can't figure out what happened," Amanda replied.

"What are we going to do?" asked another student.

"Well, I can tell you we are not doing the activity like I did it last hour," Amanda said. "Can y'all get started on the warm-up activity and let me gather a few items for the lesson?"

During the first class, Amanda had decided to videotape an activity designed to show students that there are usually several ways to solve math problems. Rather than telling the students, "This is how to solve a problem," she wanted the students to gain confidence and competence through their independent discoveries. Amanda was also introducing a unit on patterns as a precursor to an upcoming algebra unit. Unfortunately, the problem she had chosen for this particular lesson proved too difficult for students to solve by themselves, and they quickly became frustrated and resistant.

So Amanda regrouped and revamped the lesson by choosing a different problem that could be solved using skills the students would be able to apply. A few weeks before, Amanda had read James W. Stigler and James Hiebert's book, *The Teaching Gap: Best Ideas from the World's Teachers for Improving Education in the Classroom* (1999). The book analyzed the Trends in International Mathematics and Science Study (TIMSS) and the impact of Japanese lesson study. In Japan, a textbook commonly used in eighth-grade math classes is only about eighty-five pages long, much shorter than those used in most American middle schools. The Japanese teachers focus on depth of knowledge rather than a breadth of topics and use guided inquiry to help students develop increasingly sophisticated problem-solving skills. First, the teacher presents a problem to the class. Next, the students tackle the problem without assistance. Then they present their solutions to the class.

After debating the solutions, the teacher presents his or her problem-solving method and provides the answer.

With this structure in mind, Amanda decided to revise her lesson. When the students came into the classroom, Amanda said, "I like chicken wings. Anyone in here like chicken wings?

"Today we will think about chicken and try to figure out why companies like Popeye's and Raising Cane's package their buckets of chicken wings like they do. You will use your problem-solving techniques to find the number of wings that will fit in certain buckets."

The problem Amanda presented required students to apply their knowledge of multiplication and remainders to figure out the smallest number of chicken wings that could fill a bucket. Instead of having the students work in groups of four as she usually did, she paired them and asked them to solve the problem using any method they wanted. She also offered various manipulatives, including calculators and grid paper, to open problem-solving possibilities the students might not have considered.

Then, emotionally exhausted, Amanda stood back and watched, turning the responsibility for learning back to the students. "I am not answering any questions for the next twenty minutes," she said. "I want to see what you can do."

The next twenty minutes became some of the most revealing moments of Amanda's career. She began to realize that her students had many misconceptions about math that she had never noticed because usually she was doing all the talking. By allowing the students to work independently without her interference, Amanda saw their struggles and misconceptions more clearly.

Walking around the classroom, she was awed by the students' thinking, some of it on target, but much more considerably off the mark. For example, she was shocked to discover that one of her advanced students thought that a remainder of 0.3333 was the same as a remainder of 3 chicken wings. This revealed that the student had little understanding of decimals and remainders, skills she should have learned in the fourth grade.

After the students solved the chicken-wing problem by working in pairs, they shared their methods with their classmates. Some student pairs had solved the problem correctly, and some had not; but none had used the same method. Students variously used pictorial representations, counters to represent the wings, and simple calculations. Amanda did not speak until after all the students had presented their work. By this point in the class the students were on the edges of their seats, waiting to see how she would solve the problem. They were far more interested than usual because they were invested in the process. Amanda discussed her approach and then emphasized how good problem-solvers employ a variety of strategies.

Later that day, Amanda reviewed the videotaped lessons and consulted her team members.

"Okay, friends, the lesson flopped!" she said honestly.

"What? You had it planned perfectly," Monique said, smirking because she knew Amanda often blew things out of proportion.

"No, it really sunk the first hour, but the second class was terrific!"

"What did you do differently?" asked Monique.

"I changed the problem," Amanda answered, her enthusiasm building. "I also made some changes in how I interacted with the students, mainly by not talking. I didn't help while they were solving the problem. I just shut up."

"What did they do?" asked Monique.

"They went to work," Amanda said. "Then I let each pair share their solution. Some had the wrong answer but interesting methods for solution. I saved the pair with the solution using patterns until last. After it was all over, I stood up and discussed the solution. It was really incredible, but I am not sure why it was so much better."

"Did you ask questions as they were working?" Monique wondered.

"I did ask questions if I did not understand what they were doing, but I made sure I did not give away any judgments about their solutions."

Throughout the discussion, Amanda recognized that her silence was the catalyst for her students' exploration. As long as the students could depend on the teacher to explain how to solve the problem, they did not have to work or understand the problem for themselves. Also, the openness of the discussion built a sense of sharing that had not been present in the past. Amanda was no longer looking for a simple, correct answer but for the process students used to find the answer.

As a team we used these revelations to adapt our instruction in all classes. We realized that students needed to think and reflect, not just passively accept information from the teacher. We also understood that we needed to do a better job of encouraging open reflection throughout the team so students would feel safe to express their ideas and learn from each other. These small ideas have blossomed over the years into major themes in our teaching and teaming.

A New Perspective

We believe National Board certification is extremely beneficial, but teachers can apply many of its principles without going through the full process. Reflective teachers examine their practices and look closely at the strategies that have been successful with students and at those that might need reworking or tossing out. We view reflection as a seamless act that runs throughout our teaching moment-by-moment, day-by-day, and year-by-year. Seamless means we do not stop and say, "Okay, time to reflect for today." Rather, we are constantly analyzing our instruction and observing how our words or actions affect students individually and as a class. We make notes to ourselves and consult each other, whether in our daily lesson planners or in our team binder. Most importantly, if something goes wrong, we ask why and attempt to fix it instead of saying, "Well, this is how we have always done it."

We reflect individually, as Amanda did with the chicken-wings lesson; engage in team analysis, such as the discussions that led to better outreach to students' families; and involve students, parents, administrators, and community members in our ongoing deliberations. If we want to improve, we have to continually and collectively focus on results.

Before Kathryn joined our team, she had experienced lesson reflection as an academic exercise. During her teacher preparation program and student teaching stints, she was expected to critique her instruction regularly, rating her students' understanding, comprehension, and academic success. Still, she thought the process was too one-sided and yearned for more guidance from educators who routinely observed her in action.

In her first year at Dutchtown Middle School, Kathryn often wandered over to our team area and listened to the discussions during our common planning period. She noted that routinely analyzed our instruction and assessments. Even during the last week of school, our conversations focused on lesson design, implementation, and what we could improve next time.

The following school year, when Kathryn officially joined the team, our reflections became even more nuanced and insightful. She was particularly adept at analyzing student interactions in the classroom. For example, she helped us understand a subtle negative interaction between two students.

"Have you noticed in your class that when Mark is absent, Alan completes his work faster?" Kathryn asked one day.

"Now that you say that," replied Monique, "You're right. He is more focused."

"They don't sit together, so what's the deal?" asked Amanda.

"A few weeks ago when Alan made a better grade, I noticed that Mark was pretty mean to him," said Kathryn.

"Maybe we need to look into this a bit further and talk to Mark and Alan," said Amanda.

"I think we should also find a way to build Mark's confidence while encouraging Alan to perform," Monique suggested. "We may also think about moving Mark to the other group."

By bringing up what she'd noticed about the subtle dynamics at play between these two students, Kathryn had helped us make an improvement where we hadn't realized we needed one.

As we continued working together and analyzing our practices, we also began sharing our plans for future lessons and asking for ideas about how we might tweak the intended approach. We also made it part of the team's routine to discuss our lessons in progress to gain deeper insights about what we could change during the next class period or the following day.

"Goodness," Amanda said one day, as she plopped in a chair to begin our team debriefing. "That was terrible! No one got the lesson today. They are clueless."

"No one?" asked Monique skeptically.

"Okay, some did, but most are still making careless errors. I mean, they have been subtracting fractions since the fourth grade!"

"So where is the breakdown in the process?" asked Kathryn.

"Well, I think most are making their mistakes when they have to borrow from the whole number, which I know is a difficult process. But I am really not sure what's going on."

"What can you relate this to that may help them understand?" asked Monique.

"I thought I had related it with the multitude of examples and the manipulatives and using the paper plates," said Amanda, almost losing her patience.

"Maybe you could have them verbally share the process and talk about the whys," Monique suggested.

"Or you could have them write an explanation of a problem like you did with the equations last year," Kathryn said. "That was really revealing."

"You know, that is a really good idea," Amanda said, brightening. "Then maybe I could show my written explanation and pair them up to discuss the similarities and differences between their explanation and mine. I would then have time to walk around the classroom and read the individual responses. I could also probably fix the issues of the ones who just have a simple misconception."

"If you do that, then I could pull aside those students who really don't get it and work with them one on one," said Kathryn.

As helpful as these discussions are, collegial conversations sometimes don't go far enough. Sometimes seeing is the best way to understand what's working or collapsing in the classroom. Often in the past few years, one of us has popped next door to ask, "Hey, can you come watch me teach this little section and see what you think?"

Three teachers in two classrooms is a blessing because at least one of us is always available if the other two need to team up to observe a lesson or to coteach. The observing teacher's perspective is so valuable, whether she notices the impact of a particular classroom configuration or the too-small font size used during a PowerPoint presentation. We never cease to be amazed at what a fresh pair of eyes can bring to our reflections.

Our openness with colleagues carries over to our students as well. They hear us discussing teaching and watch us learning on the job. Our willingness to wrestle with challenging intellectual and practical problems demonstrates the importance of reflection and the benefits of teamwork.

When a new student or teacher joins our team, we explain our expectations and routines and then let modeling reinforce those messages. However, as the old saying goes, "You can lead a horse to water, but you can't make him drink." Internal motivation is key to reflective learning. And the best inspiration for trying something new or difficult is watching someone else succeed.

Kathryn learned that one of the cardinal rules on our team was devoting twenty minutes a day to sustained silent reading. She also discovered that Amanda and Monique read alongside students, modeling good reading habits. Initially, Kathryn resisted. Having recently graduated from college where all of her reading was for assignment purposes, she had gotten away from reading for pleasure and personal growth. During the reading period, she would quietly complete special education paperwork, file documents, check and respond to email messages—anything but read. That is, until the day she noticed that students always approached Monique and Amanda when they had questions or discoveries about reading. No one sought advice from Kathryn, and that got her thinking: "The times that students approach teachers for advice or just to talk are few and far between. If reading is what brings about more of these opportunities, then I better jump on board!"

In addition to her desire to have more personal interactions with students, Kathryn realized she needed to read more to grow professionally. She often felt clueless when Amanda and Monique would discuss the latest trends and research in education. Because she was unfamiliar with an author's work, Kathryn would listen to Amanda and Monique's discussions about new "best practices" and how they could be implemented into the classrooms. She asked good questions, but it wasn't the same as if she had read the information herself and could deepen the discussion. She became determined to change.

The second nine weeks in language arts class that year began with a study of *The Outsiders*. Kathryn obtained a copy of the book for herself, and every day during the twenty-minute silent period she read it when the students did. Within a few days, students were buzzing about her, asking for her opinions about various characters and plot developments and sharing their own interpretations. Kathryn also made sure to be in Monique's classroom on the days set aside for literature sharing circles so she could contribute to the class discussion. Kathryn made such a habit of reading daily that when the novel study came to an end she continued reading in class as well as twenty minutes at night, meeting the same requirements that our team had set for students.

After establishing a routine of reading daily for pleasure, Kathryn began reading for professional development. Sometimes she chose short online journal articles; other times she evaluated research-based strategies as part of a book study. In addition to sharing with Amanda and Monique, she began consulting other faculty members. No one forced her or twisted her arm. Kathryn developed internal motivation because our team cultivated purposeful and habitual reading.

Dissection and Reconstruction

Our dedication to professional growth and reflection extends beyond the classroom. We attend national and regional conferences and join online book studies. When we discover innovative and successful practices anywhere, we contact the teachers and administrators and ask, "How do you do that?" We write grants and seek experts to help us solve problems.

Effective teachers are continuous learners. We often have heard our colleagues remark, "I am a math teacher, I don't read," or "When do you have time to talk about research?" In order to constantly be refreshed and grow, teachers must learn.

In the book *Reflective Teaching: An Introduction*, Kenneth M. Zeichner and Daniel P. Liston write that "if a teacher never questions the goals and the values that guide his or her work, the context in which he or she teaches, or never examines his or her assumptions, then it is our belief that this individual is not engaged in reflective teaching" (1996, 1).

Recall from the chicken-wing math problem that Amanda did not continue with the lesson and wait until later to correct the problems. Losing valuable time with students because of an inadequate lesson was simply unacceptable. Instead, she reflected and regrouped immediately. We know our lessons can always be better, and we are not afraid to admit that we may not know how to improve them on our own.

Sometimes reflecting causes us to change our beliefs as well as our instruction. In Amanda's case, she recalled being an avid math hater until she reached the seventh grade and discovered Mrs. Donahue's dynamic teaching, which included using humor and relating math to real life. Mrs. Donahue made math interesting by connecting complex concepts to simple skills, which made them easier to remember.

Once she decided to become a math teacher herself, Amanda vowed that she would never use the boring, "kill and drill" exercises that had turned her off as a student. Instead, she would focus on problem-solving and math discussions, trying to recreate the stimulating classes she remembered from middle school.

Much later, she realized that effective teaching isn't based solely on the instructor's personal preferences. Rather, skillful teachers vary their tools according to students' needs. One year, for example, while examining her students' end-of-year test scores, Amanda discovered that they had an average of 87 percent in problem-solving but only 57 percent in number operations. She also noticed that students at the lower end of the spectrum consistently underperformed on number operations. These gaps suggested that Amanda had succeeded in showing students how to apply their mathematical knowledge, but they still lacked some basic skills. Many students couldn't compute easily or automatically. On tests, they took so long to complete calculations that they fell behind and never finished all the problems. Amanda reluctantly considered incorporating some old-fashioned computational speed drills two or three times a week as a way to help students to learn their basic facts. She was not sure this would improve students' skills, but she was willing to try it.

Kathryn also helped us see that our special education students would require additional interventions. During a team discussion, she asked, "How can we help the special education students improve without making them feel singled out?" We all remembered the look on the face of the kid from our own school years who performed poorly on drills.

These two incidents caused us to begin reflecting about the role and importance of math speed drills. After much discussion, Amanda created a new system. During the first week of school the students took a five-minute pencil-and-paper diagnostic test consisting of sixty-eight integer basic facts, which would establish a baseline for measuring future progress.

Each time the students participated in a drill, they had to answer at least one more problem correctly than they had on the previous drill in order to earn a point. At the end of the quarter Amanda added the improvement points and awarded a comparable grade. For example, if a student improved twenty times in twenty-five drills, he or she would earn a grade of 80 percent. The math classes also competed with each other to see which could collectively improve the most. Students who consistently scored between 60 and 68 points (68 being the top score) earned bonus points that they could use to bolster an exam score or to replace some homework assignments.

Walt scored 13 out of 68 points the first day. He was really irritated to discover that two of his friends had earned perfect scores and received certificates to be placed on the bulletin board. But the desire to reach the same level motivated Walt to work harder, and two weeks later he also earned a perfect score.

"Wow, Walt, I am so proud of you," said Amanda, "Tell me your secret."

"Well Mrs. Mayeaux, I go home every day and watch *Little House on the Prairie*," said Walt.

The connection seemed so ludicrous that Amanda couldn't help but chortle.

"Hey, stop laughing," Walt said, smiling too. "That is one nice little show."

When Amanda asked for more explanation, Walt told her that "durin' the commercials, I take out my flash cards and I mute the TV and go through the cards. I then tell myself, 'Walt, you are so smart. Here I am, perfect score.'"

Eureka! He had learned to visualize success and internalize the same positive messages we had sent him through the team. Kathryn heard the tail end of the conversation.

"I am so pleased," she told Walt. "I think I will give you a new task. I would like for you to help Mary. If you can help her score at least 50 out of 68, I will give you ten bonus points. But you have to be nice." The final reminder was added because Walt on occasion liked to tease girls.

If Amanda had never reexamined her beliefs in light of compelling evidence and Kathryn had not considered our special education students' needs, we might not have noticed that our team wasn't achieving to its fullest potential. Amanda's initial decision to eliminate a potentially successful teaching technique was based on emotion, not fact. She didn't like math computation drills as a student, so she assumed that everyone else would hate them too. She never considered the role that drilling plays in skill development. Our reflection allowed us to identify the problems and make adjustments to better serve our students.

Evidence of Mastery

Every reflection of teaching should address two main questions:

1. Did the instruction or assessment improve learning?

2. What evidence proves this is true?

Expecting teachers to demonstrate the impact of their decisions and practices can be intimidating and difficult to quantify. Typically, many of us just grade students' papers and tests and consider the results sufficient documentation of knowledge. In reality, the grades reflect how well students carried out our assignments, not necessarily how much they know about a topic or what they can do with the information later. Truly understanding the depth of their comprehension requires a different approach.

The National Board certification process helped us shift to an evidentiary focus, which teaming supports. Now as we plan instruction, we ask the following questions:

- What are my goals for this unit?
- How will students demonstrate mastery?
- What does mastery look like?
- How will the unit develop deeper knowledge of the subject content and standards?
- How will the unit build on students' prior learning?
- How can we relate this learning to other subjects?

Then, as we analyze students' work throughout the unit, we seek similar clarification:

- What evidence did the student provide to demonstrate mastery?
- Did the student build on prior learning? How do I know?
- What connections did the student make that I did not anticipate?
- What misconceptions does the student still have?

In addition to analyzing products and demonstrations from students, we examine the instruction that preceded those products and demonstrations. Two of the most powerful research tools include videotaping and peer observations. Monique and Amanda both had to videotape lessons for National Board certification. They realized after watching the lessons that they did almost all of the talking in class, while students did very little. Through the years, we all have worked hard to reverse the ratios. We now videotape ourselves at least a few times a year to reflect on a new lesson or an old one that is not working well anymore. We may watch the tapes together or individually. We keep our reflection questions at the forefront of our minds as we decide what needs to change.

We also observe each other in action. Amanda had been reading some research about the effective schools movement and was curious about whether or not the percentage of our students who were on task at any given time matched the recommended minimum level of 75 percent. She popped into Monique's class a few times to measure. We found that overall 95 percent of our students were on task at a given time. Of course we then tried to figure out what the other 5 percent were doing!

Videotaping and peer observation require trust. Just as when building relationships with students, we suggest starting slowly. Consider taping a segment of a lesson that needs tweaking and ask your teammates to offer one suggestion. Banish the idea that everything has to be perfect.

In addition, keep in mind that reflection shouldn't stop with the teacher. We encourage our students to analyze their work as well as critique their peers' work, using constructive criticism as another method for learning. Initially, students may be hesitant to critique each other, but they will get more comfortable with the process through practice and coaching.

Journal writing can be a good place to start. Asking students to reflect on their learning by writing brief explanations to a peer often loosens them up. We might ask, "How does your understanding of "Nothing Gold Can Stay" change the implications of *The Outsiders* for you?" or "How does understanding the Pythagorean theorem help you solve the refrigerator problem more efficiently?" Written exchanges are less personal and can create openings for discussion. As the year progresses, we guide students toward more face-to-face analysis.

We also share our own lesson reflections with students and ask for their advice. We might prompt them by saying, "You know, last hour this lesson flopped, so I am going to take a few minutes to change it around, and we will see if it works better. I would like to know what you think." Or, we might ask the class to give us a short written critique of a new strategy we used. Our students see us reflecting and adopt the habit as well.

End of Year Survey—Personal Growth and Reflection

Look over the work you have accumulated in your portfolio this year and answer the following questions in complete statements.

1. How have you changed as a learner? Give an example to explain your response.

   I have changed as a learner because I learned to make connections when the teachers teach. Once they dressed up as pirates and made the pirate theme go in all classes. In math we did pirate problems. In English we did piracy on the computer. Like you shouldn't just copy the paragraph you have to make it your own. In social studies we learned about Pirates. Modern day and in the olden days.

2. List three concepts, techniques, strategies, etc. that you will use again next school year. What makes these stand out?

   I used SPLAT in ELA. It helped me to write my essay questions in complete paragraphs. Keeping the table of contents up and with what we do, helped me keep track of my notes.

3. How have your reading habits changed this year? What evidence is provided by your portfolio to support this change?

   My reading habits have changed this year because reading 20min. in class and 20min at night really helps reading if you are wanting to read faster. My reading chart proves I read more books toward the end of the year than the beginning because I only read 3 books at the beginning of the year and 7 at the end.

Figure 8.1 End-of-Year Growth and Reflection Survey

At the end of the school year, our students analyze their cumulative learning by completing the survey shown in Figure 8.1 and reviewing collected work samples. Such self-reflection reinforces the importance of retaining what you've learned, not discarding it at the completion of a unit or test. By

4. What areas do you need to improve upon? What will you do next year to address these issues?

I need to improve on math problems. Like setting up proportions. I will ask questions next year and not just assume the answers.

5. What did we do this year that really made you think?

Something that made me think was the Giant Activity in math. We had to find out how heavy he was, What his hieght was, and how old he was just by measuring his foot print on the wall.

6. What do you want your parents and teachers to know about this school year?

What I want my parents and teachers to know about the best school year in middle school is the teachers are awesome and have to be my teachers next year. I also want them to know that they really are teachers because they make stuff click with things you do in real life, and make learning fun.

Figure 8.1 continued

returning to their portfolios and talking about their growth, students realize that knowledge is progressive and that each new element represents a step toward deep comprehension.

At the end of the year we often hear comments such as the following:

"Look at this stuff from August. I can't believe I thought I could not fill up a page."

"I can't believe I read thirty books this year."

"Wow, look how easy these math problems were. I don't know why I thought it was hard."

We designed the end-of-the-year surveys for our students' benefit, but the information they share also helps us improve our teaching. The student reflections become a major portion of our summer team analysis, and we continue to receive reviews long after students leave our classrooms.

"Mrs. Mayeaux, you need to add more homework because we have so much in high school," one student wrote to us from high school.

"We need to know how to use a science textbook better because that is all we use this year," another student urged.

Our students grow from watching us grow. They also help us walk our talk.

Because of rapid growth in Dutchtown Middle School's enrollment, the administrators recently decided it was best to have students move from class to class in single file, escorted by their teachers. This was an unwelcome change for many students and teachers. Monique was especially upset by the new policy, and though she tried to hide her discomfort from the students, she was unsuccessful in the attempt. She struggled at first with remembering to pick the students up from their elective classes to line them up for the end-of-the-day walk to the school buses.

One day Taylor said, "Mrs. Wild, if it's such a problem for you, then don't do it. I bet no one would even notice us not being in a line."

Monique paused for a moment, turned to Taylor, and calmly replied, "Yes Taylor, it is a problem for me because it's something I have never had to do in my years of teaching middle school. However, I have a boss who has given us new instructions to follow, and even though it's something I'm not happy about, I will follow those instructions."

Coincidentally, the following day in language arts class, Monique was explaining to Taylor that parts of the integrated Civil War assignment required independent research. He was not happy about the criteria and spent about five minutes trying to persuade Monique to just give him the answers. Finally, in exasperation, he said, "Okay, Mrs. Wild, this is a pain for me because I've never had to do all the research myself. But you're my boss, so I guess I have to follow your instructions even when I'm not happy about it."

Of course, he said this while smiling and mocking Monique's voice from the day before. Monique couldn't help but appreciate how well he had internalized the message from her previous modeling: Don't quit just because you disagree with a decision.

Together We Grow

A teaching team is only as good as the sum of its parts. Stressed and burned-out teachers don't benefit anyone. Effective teams understand the need for personal rejuvenation. They look after one another.

One recent weekend Amanda received a phone call from a colleague who asked if she could drop by the house to chat. Soon after she arrived, the friend burst into tears.

"I need to know how to do this," she said. "School is taking over my life. My family doesn't even want me to mention school anymore, but this is what I do. I am a teacher. I can't separate this from who I am, and I need to be able to share what is going on. How do you do this?"

Many aspects of teaching can cause us to feel overwhelmed and occasionally lead us to despair. And, as this teacher's remarks indicated, it can be difficult to find someone who truly understands our job's challenges.

Teammates can stop us from feeling devastated by a failure and show us how to achieve the next success. If your teammates are showing signs of wear and tear, tell them. Then offer suggestions for getting out of the slump. The following is some of the advice we've offered to each other over the years:

- Give your family a break. Have a "no-school-talk" time or a "no-school" night. Perhaps you can play board games together on Tuesdays or go out to eat on Thursdays. During that time, you need to focus on your family. Leave school at school.
- Find some time alone.
- Do something good for yourself such as exercising, getting a massage, or just sitting on a porch swing and humming. When you feel calm, your students will follow your lead.
- Laugh with your teammates every day!

- Go ahead, have a good cry. We won't tell. We'll provide the tissues to mop your eyes and provide the shoulders to lean on.
- Connect with friends and activities outside of school. We are currently reading *East of Eden* with our "smart women" group. We like the brain-stretch without the education chat.

Teaching is always on our minds, but sometimes we come up with our best ideas when we leave the job behind. We might go to the movies and find a surprising connection to an upcoming unit or read the newspaper on a Saturday morning and catch a related article. We never totally turn off our teacher brains, but we've learned how to shift into lower gears.

When Amanda began teaching at Pickering Elementary in Pickering, Louisiana, the principal, Dr. Cynthia Gillespie, stood up at the year's first faculty meeting and said, "I am so glad you have chosen our school. I like teachers who smile. I don't like teachers who lug home tons of work every night and stay until dark every day because those teachers will be too exhausted to smile by December. Have a life, and you will always love teaching."

Work smarter, not harder. We maximize our planning time by getting work done. If you have to grade papers at home, make a schedule. Tell your family, "I have to grade papers Tuesday night, but on Wednesday I am free," or "This is the end of the nine weeks; I will be a bit crazy this week." As a new teacher, learn tricks for managing paperwork such as assigning numbers to students so you can quickly organize their papers. Pay attention to your calendar. Don't wait until the last week of the grading period to assign three five-page essays.

Finally, don't overlook your students as resources. We'll never forget the year that Amanda and Monique both went to graduate school and Kathryn had to complete the requirements for the state's new teacher assessment program. Periodically, we would practice our graduate school presentations in front of our students so they would see what our professional work looked like and understand that we too had to demonstrate to peers. We shared our professors' critiques and our multiple revisions. Crystal, one of our students, was profoundly affected. At the end of the school year, she shared these thoughts in her journal: "When I grow up I want to be a woman like you. You do it all. You have a great family and a home and a career, but you still keep learning. I think that is what makes you happy. I want to be happy."

Example is our greatest teacher. Our students know we value learning because we learn. Our students reflect because we reflect. Whether we demonstrate a Sudoku solution or simply write "What I am reading" on the whiteboard, our students are watching. Don't miss the reflection.

ChapterNine
Catch Them Before They Fall

Gareth was a Dennis the Menace type with precious dimples and a quick smile. He was in our classes only a few days before we held the first team conference about his behavior. Although Gareth was driving us crazy, he was so good-natured and funny that we found it very difficult not to laugh at his antics along with our other students. Because Gareth was on the middle school football team, we could report his behavior to the coaches as a way to keep him in line.

Amanda taught three math classes and one extended block of language arts that year, which meant that she had the pleasure of working with Gareth and his good friend, Carl, for three hours a day. Through horseplay, teasing, and dozens of other distracting behaviors, Gareth and Carl tried to avoid every reading activity Amanda introduced. Finally, we invited Gareth's parents to a team conference.

Gareth's father, a six-foot-five-inch bear of a man, entered the classroom and flashed a smile as broad as his son's. During the conference, we learned that Gareth's mother was bedridden and waiting for a transplant while his father worked nights to support the family. Gareth's dad, a first-generation high school graduate, told us that he would do whatever he could to help us get his son on track. He also shared that as part of an African American family living in an all-white suburban neighborhood, Gareth had had a difficult time fitting into his new surroundings. He preferred to visit Carl and his family, who lived in a distant public housing project.

We discussed how we might use these insights to strengthen our relationships with Gareth and felt hopeful that his father would support our efforts in the classroom. A few days later, however, after Gareth caused another disturbance, Amanda held him back during lunch.

"I have really reached the end of my rope with you," Amanda said. "I ask you to read and you clown. Why?"

Gareth mumbled and averted his eyes.

"You have to speak up if you want me to hear you," Amanda said, now fully exasperated.

Gareth looked up at his teacher and spoke slowly, "I can't read, and neither can Carl."

Amanda remembers this moment as one of the most shocking of her career. How could she not have noticed the boys' illiteracy? How had Gareth and Carl made it to the eighth grade with such glaring deficiencies? And now that Gareth had revealed his secret, what was our team going to do about it?

Amanda reached out to Gareth and extended a mutual challenge. "If I can teach you to read, will you stop driving everyone crazy?" she asked.

Gareth agreed, and the deal was set into motion. Amanda went to Monique who suggested the book, *A Taste of Blackberries*, which is written on a low reading level but is still a high-interest story for young adolescents. Amanda asked the school's speech therapist for a reading diagnostic test so she would know which literacy skills to pinpoint first. The test revealed several gaps for both boys, especially their ability to comprehend text and read fluently. Gareth's word-recognition skills were adequate, but he did not understand what he was reading. Carl could decode only basic words.

Amanda pulled the boys aside during reading class to work with them one on one with a few simple reading strategies tailored to their needs. For Gareth, Amanda focused on his mental conceptualization of the story by having him read a passage aloud and then discuss what he "saw" in his mind. For homework, she asked him to draw pictures of these mental images and write short summaries of the text.

Carl's problems were more complex. He began working with the Dolch sight-word list that Amanda had saved from her younger daughter's class. Amanda put the words on flash cards, and Carl used these to develop rapid recognition skills. Amanda also built on both boys' decoding skills by teaching them to use context clues to understand text rather than getting hung up on one word at a time. This improved both boys' fluency. As Carl's basic skills improved, Amanda added some of the comprehension strategies she had selected for Gareth.

Within a few weeks, both boys had finished the book and were proud of their accomplishment. Throughout the year, they read many more books, along with stories, poems, speeches, and articles. Gareth and Carl often stayed after school with our team to complete homework or get extra help. At the end of the school year, both boys passed the state assessment, reaching the proficient level in all subjects, although Carl scored at the lowest level of proficient in reading. Gareth sent a letter of thanks to Amanda and promised to invite her to his high school graduation.

During the next two years, Gareth occasionally stopped by to see us. He played football his freshman year, and his mom got a transplant. Although Gareth still misbehaved now and then, he passed all of his classes and seemed to be doing fine.

One afternoon, toward the end of Gareth's sophomore year in high school, Amanda looked up from her shopping cart at the supermarket and saw Gareth approaching. After exchanging hugs and marveling at Gareth's towering height, Amanda asked about school.

"I quit," Gareth said sheepishly and avoided her gaze.

"What?" Amanda gasped. "I thought you were passing!"

"I was, but I just don't belong there, and it was so boring," he said. "I am going to get a GED, maybe, and do something else. It doesn't matter."

The Students Behind the Statistics

In education we say that every student matters. We vow that no child will be left behind. So why are we still losing so many students like Gareth?

As politicians, researchers, journalists, educators, and parents endlessly debate the causes and consequences of staggering school dropout rates, students like Gareth continue to fall through the cracks. According to the National Center for Education Statistics, just 75 percent of U.S. students who enter ninth grade graduate from high school four years later. In Louisiana, that figure drops to 69.4 percent. High school dropouts account for 75 percent of state prison inmates and 59 percent of federal prison inmates (Harlow 2002). High school dropouts cost the U.S. government $24 billion annually in lost economic opportunity, social welfare benefits, and increased crime (Thorstensen 2005).

Traditionally research cited poverty, race, and socioeconomic factors as barriers to graduation. We do not dispute these findings, but recently we came across a new study that interviewed students to find out when and why they left school. *The Silent Epidemic*, a report sponsored by the Bill and

Melinda Gates Foundation (Bridgeland, DiIulio, and Morison 2006), painted a different picture of dropouts. Among the surprising top reasons that students gave for checking out early were the following:

- Their classes were not interesting (47 percent).
- They had missed too many days of school and could not catch up (43 percent).
- They spent time with people who were not interested in school (42 percent).
- They had too much freedom and not enough rules (38 percent).
- They were failing in school (35 percent).

It's sobering information, to be sure, but also quite hopeful. Think about it for a moment. Most of those reasons are within our power to change. We can combat those negative forces and get students back on track to succeed. Teaming provides us with a solid battle plan.

Did we hear grumbling in the background? Impatient sighs? Are your arms crossed defiantly across your chest? These are natural reactions to the staggering responsibility before us, but we urge you to resist the impulse to quit or cast aspersions.

As middle grades educators, it's easy to place the blame for student failure on high school teachers who may not extend the system of supports that we strive to provide. High school teachers, in turn, can just as quickly find fault with the way students were prepared in the middle grades. We're not interested in playing this game of pin the blame on the scapegoat, because it distracts us from the problem. Every teacher at every level of education shapes the successes and failures of students. And if we don't start working together to plug the gaps, we will continue to lose students before they've had a chance to reach their full potential.

A crucial part of the process has to do with understanding why students drop out of school. *The Silent Epidemic* offers some important clues. Let's consider each of the students' stated reasons in turn.

Classes Were Not Interesting

As previously discussed in Part II, our students tell us they enjoy our team because we make our classes fun, but they also say they try harder in school because they get to do "real work" on our team. As we examine effective methods to keep students engaged in education, we must consider the critical combination of academic rigor, high expectations, and purposeful learning. Middle grades students, who are on the cusp of independence, need to feel capable of completing increasingly complex assignments that are connected to the world beyond the classroom. Relevance may be a new education buzzword, but it's still essential to academic success. "Keepin' it real" must become our mantra as we design instruction and assessments that truly matter instead of merely enable us to cover the curriculum or fill the grade book. Students want to see how their educational experiences pertain to the rest of their lives, which is why so many reform models for high school focus on career applications.

As a team, we hold each other accountable for the rigor and high expectations of all classes. We have a deep understanding of our individual subject specialties, but we also know each other's content. We review lessons and assessments for evidence of engagement and authentic connections. Would anyone ever write the sterile business letter to Mr. Brown that's reprinted on page 121 of the grammar book? No! But people often need to communicate with companies and organizations. So why don't we explore some real issues that students care about—product defects, career information, new technology, and the like—and show them how to write a formal letter to express their intentions and get responses?

As administrators, school districts, and state and federal policymakers search for ways to help students and teachers reach higher expectations, they should look to teaming for an effective system of checks and balances. We may not be able to change the circumstances that shape our students' lives outside of school, but we can change what they experience in our classrooms. By feeding them a rich intellectual diet of collaborative, engaging, and purposeful activities, we will lose fewer students to boredom and irrelevance.

Missed Too Many Days and Could Not Catch Up

As a team, we attack absenteeism every day because we know that students are more likely to do well when they attend school on a regular basis. Kathryn is the attendance queen. She monitors attendance throughout the team and tracks absenteeism by sending email messages, making phone calls, writing letters, and talking to students when they return. The consistent follow-through is a strong deterrent to truancy. When families fail to respond, we don't hesitate to contact the school district's truancy officer.

Our administrators expect us to be accountable for students. We had better know why Suzy has missed five days in a row, and we must have the documentation to prove that we tried to contact her family. We also have high standards of achievement, which we repeatedly convey to students so Suzy and her peers understand why it matters that they attend school regularly. In addition to setting the bar high, we try to encourage good attendance by providing engaging lessons and exciting team activities. Basically, students do not want to miss the fun.

Spent Time with People Not Interested in School

Although we can't choose the people our students associate with before and after school, we can create a team culture that will positively influence their decisions. On our team we use peer mentoring and buddy systems daily in our classes for several reasons. By mentoring one another, the students begin to depend on each other and form bonds. The bonds are beginning connections we will use to strengthen the team. The mentor feels needed and the mentee feels supported. The roles do not remain concrete but may reverse as needed. We also strategically team students to break down personality issues and cliques that may have been present during previous school years. The students also improve communication skills and teamwork skills. As students form new friendships, those relationships often carry over to after-school activities and into high school.

We also bring in outside speakers to talk about their experiences and encourage students to make wise decisions. One of our most successful visitors was Darry Beckwith, a Louisiana State University football standout and one of our former students. Darry stressed the importance of character. He said that when Coach Nick Saban came to recruit him in high school, he talked to Darry's teachers first to find out about his work ethic and character.

Other visitors, such as the state game warden mentioned previously, share how classroom learning relates to real-world issues and careers. Regardless of their occupations, the speakers share the same message: "You are judged by whom you hang out with, and your future will be shaped by your decisions today."

We also use classroom lessons to reinforce these points. For example, we often read *The Outsiders* by S. E. Hinton and reflect on the fictional characters' struggles with gang initiation and personal loyalty. The novel helps us frame deep discussions about how our social circles define us.

Sometimes we have to walk a fine line. While trying to elevate our students' aspirations and broaden their worldviews, we cannot be judgmental of their families or neighborhoods. Rather, we model civility and respectful behavior so they will see the benefits of treating people fairly. In turn, they start expecting better of and for themselves.

Teaming can be a catalyst for changing a school's entire culture. When we break down the walls that isolate students and keep them from forming strong attachments, we discover why positive relationships help adolescents stay in school. Every student wants to belong, and teaming builds on that basic human instinct by providing a safe and comfortable place to learn.

Had Too Much Freedom and Not Enough Rules

Many of our students come from homes with limited structure. When they join our team, they often have heard about the fun activities we do but incorrectly associate the promise of enjoyment with anarchy. They don't expect us to focus on discipline. Many students are surprised by our strict requirements for daily reading and the proper procedure for writing math solutions. We have high expectations for all students, and we do not lower those goals.

Shockingly, students usually accept our terms and fall in line. We have few chronic behavior problems. Why? Rules! We explain, practice, and reinforce our expectations constantly. On our team, the rules are the same all day, every day. Students know what to do and revel in the consistency. Young adolescents experience enough upheaval because of their rapid physical, emotional, and intellectual development. They draw comfort from the constancy of a collaborative team.

Structure is crucial to students' success. If your school is in chaos and the classes seem in shambles, consider your procedures and expectations. How should students move from class to class? Does at least one adult know where each student is throughout the school day? How can students find out about missed assignments when they are absent? Who will be responsible for sharing the news that Jim's grandmother died and how that might affect his behavior in class? Teaming enables us to ask and answer those questions daily.

Was Failing in School

If you ask pedestrians on the street to describe a dropout, many will say a student who hasn't passed all of his or her classes. Perhaps many teachers also believe that to be true. Why quit if you are being successful? But surprisingly, the majority of dropouts were not failing prior to leaving school. In *The Silent Epidemic* survey, 65 percent of dropouts were passing, and 88 percent of those had a C average or better. The survey also found that 65 percent of the dropouts surveyed agreed that "at least one teacher on campus personally cared about my success." This statement gave us pause until we considered that many students might need more than one trusted adult to light the way. When teams work well, every student should be able to say, "All of my teachers personally care about my success."

Belonging, vision, and purpose are powerful motivators. In large schools with random classroom assignments, students can easily get lost in the crowd. Teachers who are responsible for 150 students a day have a difficult time connecting with students on a personal level and holding each one to high standards.

As a team we place high priority on the nonacademic aspects of school. We want our students to belong to our team and know we are personally committed to their success. As we work through the year, we help students frame a vision for the future by setting goals and reflecting on their strengths and weaknesses. We do not accept answers such as "I just can't" or "I dunno." We are not afraid to ask, "Why did you fail this?" "Why did you not do your reading?" or "Where were you yesterday?" We also try to highlight progress and each team member's contributions so every student will know he or she has a purpose.

Teaming enables multiple shepherds to keep the lambs from going astray. As a team, our daily notes, observations, and communications about students help us spot trends or possible issues. We do not wait until the nine-week term is over and look at failing grades to find a child in trouble. We know that low or declining grades are seldom the first indication of trouble.

We know what our students' issues are because we have personal relationships with them and recognize when something is amiss. Through our daily anecdotal notes where we reference missed homework, declining math scores, negative behavior, and many other cues, we continually look out for students who may need more attention. We then can act upon those issues before failure has time to take hold. Our interventions may be as simple as setting up a team conference with the students and their families or recommending after-school tutoring. Many times, just sharing our understanding that adolescence is a tremendously challenging time for students is enough to help them cope.

Extending Teaming Beyond the Middle Grades

Teaming in high school? Yes! We are excited to see more secondary schools recognizing the benefits of teaming as a supportive organizational structure, particularly at the freshman level.

In Louisiana, the Board of Elementary and Secondary Education is implementing tough high school redesign policies. Much of the process centers on improving high school freshmen's experiences. In our opinion, these changes are long overdue. We are always surprised and disillusioned when we discover that one of our formerly successful students dropped out or failed classes in the ninth grade.

For example, Louisa left us with a B average in math and a score that placed her in the sixty-eighth percentile on the state's eighth-grade math exam. During our classes we knew that Louisa often needed extra time to complete exams and some verbal encouragement, but her score on the state assessment placed her firmly in the upper portion of our student population.

We were shocked to learn that she had failed Algebra I with a 14 percent average in the fall of her freshman year and again in the repeat class she took the following spring. "What happens when these kids get to high school?" we asked ourselves repeatedly. "What can we do differently to prepare them for life after middle school?"

We sought answers, of course, from the experts—our former students. The answers were not what we had expected. Although we received plenty of positive comments, the problems our students identified stood out:

"You did not give enough homework."

"You did not use the textbook enough."

"We can't use a calculator at all."

"We don't work in groups in high school."

"No one knows who I am."

While it would be easy to point fingers at high school teachers who would simply point fingers back at us, we take these comments seriously. They reveal some inconsistencies between middle school and high school and suggest the need for teachers in both grade levels to talk to each other and work together on a regular basis to smooth the transitions for students.

In Louisiana, we have been aggressively pursuing the Freshman Academy model, which recognizes the importance of providing extra academic and emotional supports for students in the ninth grade. Teaming is a crucial component of this approach.

Another high school reform model that has received national attention and supports the use of teaming is the Southern Regional Education Board's High Schools That Work initiative. High Schools That Work focuses on high expectations defined by a concise set of standards that are integrated into all classrooms. Teachers are asked to examine their practices for evidence of effectiveness and regularly seek feedback about students' learning. The focus is mastery and application of content and skills, not just high grades.

High Schools That Work also requires more math and science courses that directly relate to career and technical needs. In their junior and senior years, students are encouraged to pursue internships so they will have work experience before they graduate.

The High Schools That Work model encourages teachers to form inter-disciplinary teams, integrate curricula, and jointly analyze the quality of their lessons and assessments. Teams also must communicate their expectations to students and their families and provide support as needed. The culture is centered on continuous improvement.

There are many parallels between the key practices recommended in High Schools That Work and the statements of students who were surveyed in *The Silent Epidemic*. High school students need and desire regular opportunities for real-world learning, engaging teaching, smaller classes, better communication between home and school, and increased supervision. If we address their concerns, we will help many more students continue their education.

In our district, one high school, St. Amant High, has seen tremendous growth in the past few years by applying these principles. St. Amant High requires four years of math for all students. The teachers work together daily to increase rigor in their classes through lesson discussion and peer-evaluation of assessments. The school recently received one of the twenty national Pacesetter awards at the national High Schools That Work conference.

Our district draws further inspiration from the High Schools That Work recommendations. All four high schools recently implemented the Freshman Academy model. Like students on our middle school team, the ninth graders are placed in small learning communities with the same English, math, science, or social studies teachers. Three of the four high schools have adopted a block schedule, which enables the teams to use extended and flexible class periods.

The school district also allocated additional funds for an extra administrator, the associate principal, who works as the Freshman Academy administrator. The district hired additional teachers to trim the student/teacher ratio and provided extensive professional development for each Freshman Academy. Teachers have both personal and team planning periods every day.

We are personally invested in this model. Amanda has become the associate principal of the seventh through ninth grades at a school with a 98 percent student poverty rate and a 28 percent passing rate on the state's annual assessment. Monique has joined the same staff as one of two new master teachers who will be responsible for embedding professional development to directly address student needs.

Implementing strategies such as those recommended by High Schools That Work is difficult with a traditional mind-set. Teaming and our new, flexible schedule will give teachers time each day to strengthen their instruction as we try to move from "my classroom" to "our school community."

As an administrative team member, Amanda will depend on the daily embedded professional development to guide teachers through implementation of the school improvement plan. Just as we did on our middle school team, the Freshman Academy teams will meet daily to discuss issues, research effective strategies, analyze data, and plan for student success. We will not wait for the release of a single set of standardized test scores to tell us whether or not we have achieved our goals. We will know each day what worked and what did not because we are reflective educators.

We believe that when schools provide regular time for shared professional development within the school day, teachers find greater value in the experience. We are quickly moving away from broad and inconsistent inservice training to research-based initiatives that directly address our needs. Accountability is crucial, and administrators must also be involved.

As two of us move to a high school campus, we will not change the core beliefs that shaped our success in the middle grades. High school students do not suddenly become adults when they enter the ninth grade. They are only about ten weeks more mature than they were in the eighth grade. They still need someone to know whether or not they come to school each day, expect them to achieve greatness, hold them accountable for learning and behaving, and love them while they are growing.

When all of us in education consider ourselves members of a team, we will be able to stop focusing solely on our individual classrooms and start understanding our roles in shaping the education of the whole child. We must work together if we want to improve the productivity and culture of our nation twenty, fifty, or one hundred years from now. The future is in our hands.

ChapterTen
Final Thoughts

The positive impact that interdisciplinary teams can have on students' lives became evident to us through two chance encounters that occurred within ten minutes during a single afternoon. Monique was buying a hamburger for her son at a local church fair when a beautiful young woman approached and hugged her. Monique was taken aback. She knew this must be a former student, but she didn't immediately recognize her. While searching her memory, Monique fell back on her standby conversational icebreaker and asked whether the young woman was still in school. Instantly, the woman's eyes filled with tears.

"Oh, Mrs. Wild, you know school was never easy for me like it was for my brother, Jonas," she said.

Suddenly, Monique recalled a shy student named Angela who had struggled with reading but made great progress during her eighth-grade year.

"Well, anyway," Angela continued, "high school was not easy either. I had a baby and had to find a job to keep my baby. I didn't finish school, but I wanted you to know that on our [middle school] team I learned to read, and I could get a job because of that. Remember how our team focused on reading? Y'all taught us that if we could read, we could do anything. So I'm getting my GED. After I get my degree, I'll get a better job. I keep reading so that I can keep learning."

Angela surprised Monique with another hug and kiss. Her final words before she disappeared into the crowd were "Thanks for giving me what I need to raise my daughter. I love y'all for that."

Moments after Angela turned to leave, another former student approached Monique. Gloria was majoring in journalism at the local university and would soon graduate. She had already secured a job with the local newspaper and was quite excited about her future career. Monique knew most of this because

Gloria had excelled in middle school and still periodically stopped by to chat and fill us in on her life.

"You know, our team is the reason I want to be a writer," Gloria told Monique and her husband. "I tell everyone that."

As Gloria turned to walk away, Monique thought to herself, "Won't these encounters be something to share at our team meeting on Monday?"

Whether they are struggling or superlative, all students can find a secure place to learn on a successful team. Middle school is the ideal time to forge strong relationships, strengthen academic skills, and encourage dreams. We feel privileged to have nurtured and observed the growth of so many wonderful young adolescents during the past decade. And we will always be grateful for the personal and professional progress we made alongside them.

Teamwork is the main reason we have advanced. It created the collaborations that changed the way we view education. Teamwork taught us to appreciate differences and deepened our understanding of how every teacher and student can contribute to the academic, social, and emotional development of other team members. Teamwork showed us the wisdom of continually probing our practices for evidence of success. It required us to be vulnerable, to change ineffective habits, and to challenge our assumptions about students, their families, and our colleagues. It has not been easy, but by working together we have accomplished tasks and reached goals that initially seemed beyond our reach.

Robert Kennedy once said, "There are those who look at things the way they are, and ask why . . . I dream of things that never were, and ask why not?"

We conclude this book by asking some of our favorite collaborative "Why nots?":

- Why can't our students effect social change?
- Why can't 100 percent of our students leave school with strong literacy skills?
- Why can't children of poverty excel at the rate of their more affluent peers?
- Why can't our schools be second to none?
- Why can't our courses complement all the others to create a seamless flow of content and skills for students?
- Why can't parents be an integral part of their children's education?
- Why should teachers be secluded from one another?
- Why can't you experience the same success with teaming that we have?

Teamwork will enable you to ask and answer these and other difficult questions about our profession. Please start reflecting with your colleagues today. We will eagerly await your responses. Remember, anything is possible when you work together as a team.

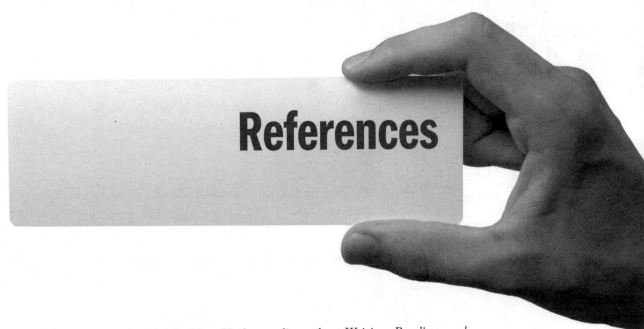

References

Atwell, Nancie. 1998. *In the Middle: New Understandings about Writing, Reading, and Learning.* 2nd ed. Portsmouth, NH: Heinemann.

Bloor, Edward. 1997. *Tangerine.* New York: Scholastic.

Breus, Michael J. 2004. "How Much Sleep Do Children Need?" http://www.webmd.com/parenting/guide/how-much-sleep-do-children-need.

Bridgeland, John M., John J. DiIulio, Jr., and Karen Burke Morison. 2006. *The Silent Epidemic: Perspectives of High School Dropouts.* Washington, DC: Civic Enterprises, in association with Peter D. Hart Research Associates for the Bill and Melinda Gates Foundation.

Dahlgren, Rick. 2005. *Time to Teach.* Hayden Lake, ID: Center for Teacher Effectiveness.

Douglass, Frederick. 1847. "If I Had a Country, I Should Be a Patriot." In *American Heritage Book of Great American Speeches for Young People.* 2001. Ed. Suzanne McIntire. New York: Wiley.

DuFour, Richard, Robert Eaker, and Rebecca DuFour, eds. 2005. *On Common Ground: The Power of Professional Learning Communities.* Bloomington, IN: National Educational Service.

Dunbar, Paul Laurence. 1899. "Sympathy." In *Norton Anthology of African American Literature*. 2003. Ed. Nellie Y. McKay and Henry Louis Gates Jr. New York: W.W. Norton.

Farr, Roger. 2002. Presentation at National Middle School Association Annual Conference, Portland, OR.

Fleischman, Paul. 1999. *Seedfolks*. New York: HarperCollins.

Flowers, Nancy, Steven B. Mertens, and Peter F. Mulhall. 1999. "The Impact of Teaming: Five Research-Based Outcomes." *Middle School Journal* 31:57–60.

Hackmann, Donald G. 1997. *Student-Led Conferences at the Middle Level, ERIC Digest*. ED 407171. Champaign, IL: ERIC Clearinghouse on Elementary and Early Childhood Education.

Hackmann, Donald G., Vicki N. Petzko, Jerry W. Valentine, Donald C. Clark, John R. Nori, and Stephen E. Lucas. 2002. "Beyond Interdisciplinary Teaming: Findings and Implications of the NASSP National Middle Level Study." *NASSP Bulletin* 86:33–47.

Harlow, Caroline Wolf. 2002. *Educational and Correctional Populations*. Washington, DC: Bureau of Justice Statistics, Office of Justice Programs.

Hesse, Karen. 2001. *Witness*. New York: Scholastic.

Hinton, S. E. 1967. *The Outsiders*. New York: Penquin.

Hunter, Madeline. 1984. "Knowing, Teaching, and Supervising." In *Using What We Know About Teaching*, ed. Philip Hosford. Alexandria, VA: Association for Supervision and Curriculum Development.

Ingersoll, Richard M. 2001. *Teacher Turnover, Teacher Shortages, and the Organization of Schools*. Seattle, WA: University of Washington, Center for the Study of Teaching and Policy.

Jackson, Anthony W., and Gayle A. Davis. 2000. *Turning Points 2000*. New York: Teachers College Press.

Jacobs, Heidi H. 1997. *Mapping the Big Picture: Integrating Curriculum and Assessment K–12*. Alexandria, VA: Association for Supervision and Curriculum Development.

———. 2004. *Getting Results with Curriculum Mapping*. Alexandria, VA: Association for Supervision and Curriculum Development.

Johnson, Susan Moore, Sarah Birkeland, Susan M. Kardos, David Kauffman, Edward Liu, and Heather G. Peske. 2001. "Retaining the Next Generation of Teachers: The Importance of School-Based Support." Harvard Education Letter Research Online. http://www.gse.harvard.edu/~ngt/.

Lesesne, Teri. 2003. *Making the Match: The Right Book for the Right Reader at the Right Time, Grades 4–12*. Portland, ME: Stenhouse.

Louisiana Administrative Code. 2005. Louisiana Content Standards, Benchmarks, and Grade Level Expectations. Available for each content area online at http://www.doa.state.la.us/osr/lac/lac28.htm.

Marzano, Robert J. 2003. *What Works in Schools: Translating Research into Action*. Alexandria, VA: Association for Supervision and Curriculum Development.

Moretti, Enrico. 2005. "Does Education Reduce Participation in Criminal Activities?" Paper presented at the symposium on the social costs of inadequate education, Teachers College, Columbia University, New York, NY.

National Center for Education Statistics. 2006. *Dropout Rates in the United States, 2004*. NCES 2007-024. Washington, DC: U.S. Department of Education.

National Commission on Teaching and America's Future. 2003. *No Dream Denied: A Pledge to America's Children*. Washington, DC: National Commission on Teaching and America's Future.

National Council of Teachers of Mathematics. 2000. *Principles and Standards for School Mathematics*. Reston, VA: National Council of Teachers of Mathematics. Available online at http://standards.nctm.org/document/appendix/alg.htm.

National Middle School Association. 2003. *This We Believe: Successful Schools for Young Adolescents*. Westerville, OH: National Middle School Association.

Roberts, Sylvia, and Eunice Pruitt. 2003. *Schools as Professional Learning Communities*. Thousand Oaks, CA: Corwin.

Roderick, Melissa. 1995. *Grade Retention and School Drop-out: Policy Debate and Research Questions*. Research Bulletin, no. 15. Bloomington, IN: Phi Delta Kappa Center for Evaluation, Development, and Research.

Rumberger, Russell W. 1995. "Dropping Out of Middle School: A Multilevel Analysis of Students and Schools." *American Educational Research Journal* 32:583–625.

Sanders, William, and Sandra Horn. 1994. "The Tennessee Value-Added Assessment System (TVAAS): Mixed Methodology in Educational Assessment." *Journal of Personnel Evaluation in Education* 8:299–311.

Scales, Peter C. 1991. *A Portrait of Young Adolescents in the 1990s: Implications for Promoting Healthy Growth and Development*. Minneapolis, MN: Search Institute.

Smith, Carol. n.d. "Assessing and Reporting Progress Through Student-Led Portfolio Conferences." http://www.nmsa.org/Publications/WebExclusive/Portfolio/tabid/650/Default.aspx.

Sousa, David A. 2005a. *How the Brain Learns to Read*. Thousand Oaks, CA: Corwin.

———. 2005b. *How the Brain Learns*. Thousand Oaks, CA: Corwin.

Southern Regional Education Board. *High Schools That Work: Key Practices*. Atlanta, GA: Southern Regional Education Board.

Stigler, James W., and James Hiebert. 1999. *The Teaching Gap: Best Ideas from the World's Teachers for Improving Education in the Classroom*. New York: The Free Press.

Stockton, Frank R. 1884. "The Lady or the Tiger." In *Interactive Reader Plus: Grade 8*. 2003. Ed. Sharon Sicinski-Skeans et al. Evanston, IL: McDougal Littell.

Sylwester, Robert. 2005. *How to Explain a Brain: An Educator's Handbook of Brain Terms and Cognitive Processes*. Thousand Oaks, CA: Corwin.

Thorstensen, Beata I. 2005. "If You Build It, They Will Come: Investing in Public Education." Albuquerque, NM: University of New Mexico. http://abec.unm.edu/resources/gallery/present/invest_in_ed.pdf.

Truth, Sojourner. 1851. "Ain't I a Woman." In *Norton Anthology of African American Literature*. 2003. Ed. Nellie Y. McKay and Henry Louis Gates Jr. New York: W.W. Norton.

U.S. Department of Education. 2000. *Twenty-Second Annual Report to Congress on the Implementation of the Individuals with Disabilities Education Act*. Washington, DC: U.S. Department of Education.

Williamson, Ronald, and J. Howard Johnston. 1999. "Challenging Orthodoxy: An Emerging Agenda for Middle Level Reform." *Middle School Journal* 30:10–17.

Wormeli, Rick. 2006. *Fair Isn't Always Equal*. Portland, ME: Stenhouse.

Zeichner, Kenneth M., and Daniel P. Liston. 1996. *Reflective Teaching: An Introduction*. Mahwah, NJ: Lawrence Erlbaum.

Index